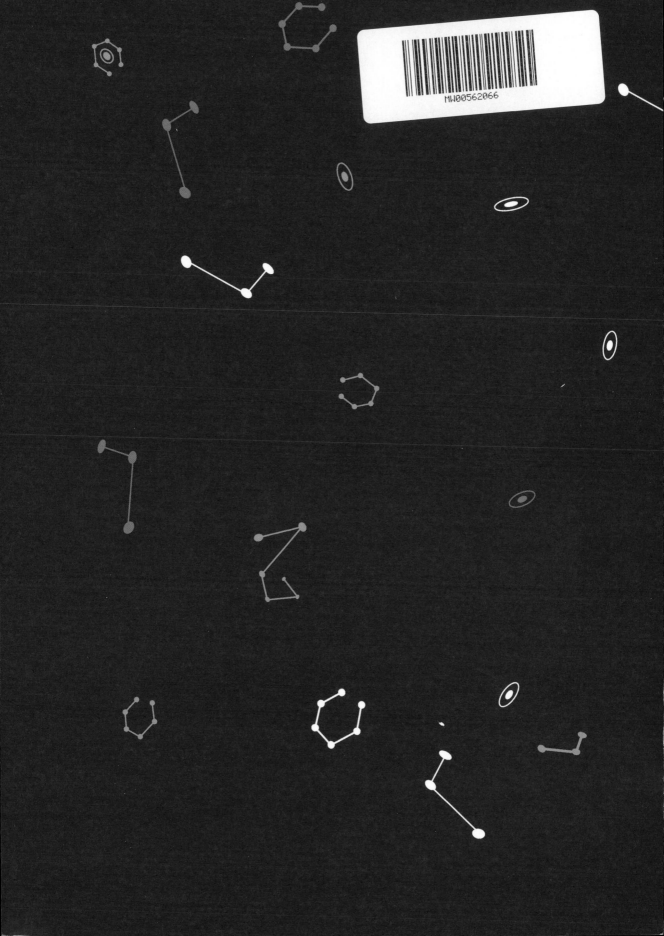

IMAGINAL CELLS: VISIONS OF TRANSFORMATION

A collection of essays that explore how a compassionate approach to business, finance, the environment and politics can transform our world.

Each essay in the publication illustrates an age-old principle of human interaction, 'The Golden Rule'. This historic belief urges people to live their lives around the simple standard of treating others as you would like to be treated.

Imaginal cells hold the vision of the butterfly. These cells consolidate – but only after the caterpillar's immune system identifies them as a threat. When they are provoked they unify, consolidate and push through their vision.

REBOOT THE FUTURE

www.rebootthefuture.org

Reboot the Future is a registered charity whose purpose is to promote the golden rule and embed it as guiding principle for business, education, society and the environment. Our goal is to encourage widespread adoption of the principle to support the shift in mindset that is needed to allow the swiftest possible adoption of the UN Sustainable Development Goals, and the transition to a more compassionate world. We are working on a number of pivotal projects to that end.

Reboot the Future's version of the Golden Rule is: Treat others and the planet the way you want to be treated.

| Curators | **KIM POLMAN AND STEPHEN VASCONCELLOS-SHARPE** |

EDITORIAL AND DESIGN

The Brewery at Freuds

Editor in Chief	**EDWARD AMORY**
Editor	**BEN JACKSON**
Executive Producer	**POPPY MITCHELL-ROSE**
Assistant Editors	**SUSANNAH MOORE AND STUART DAVIS**
Art Director	**JAMES FENTIMAN**
Design & Infographics	**MARGRIET STRAATMAN AND ALEXANDRA ZIELASKIEWICZ**
Illustrations	**JAMES FENTIMAN, JACOB VAN LEEUWEN AND ESTER VILAPLANA**

IMAGINAL CELLS:
VISIONS OF TRANSFORMATION

CONTENTS

A New Golden Era

Reimagining a shared humanity

By Kim Polman & Stephen Vasconcellos-Sharpe

HUMANKIND IS FACING CHALLENGES that raise questions over our continued stewardship of the planet.

Our generation has the potentially calamitous honour of witnessing the birth of a new era, the Anthropocene. It is an era defined by man's irreversible impacts on the world, by changes to the climate, worsening threats to eco-systems, a rapid rise in extinction rates and burgeoning levels of pollution.

A radical shift is needed for the longevity of the human race. We are at a turning point. But what principle could help propel this urgently needed change?

For over 3,000 years, one altruistic maxim has been the bedrock of humanity, underlying our most successful religions and cultures. It has been cited through the ages by prophets, religious leaders and philosophers as the guiding principle of human interaction.

THE GOLDEN RULE

Throughout history mankind has been urged to lead lives based around this simple principle. The earliest recorded mention was made by the ancient Egyptians in 1800 BC. Later, Buddha in India, Confucius in China and the Greek philosophers all wrote versions of the rule around 500 BC. Jesus established all his teachings on this basic idea: the importance of Love. Loving one's neighbour, loving your enemies.

In 610 AD, Muhammad included in the Qur'an: "Woe to those who cheat: they demand a fair measure from others but they do not give it themselves." (83:1-3). Several Hadiths clarify this: "None of you is a true believer unless he wishes for his brother what he wishes for himself."

Around the world in the following centuries leaders professed this truth: Shintoism in 700 AD in Japan, The Book of Kells in Ireland in 810, the Inca leader Manco Capac in Peru in 1200, The Tales of Sendebar in India in 1200, Sikhism in India in 1400, and many more.

Intriguingly, neuroscientists have taken this a step further, proving we become happier ourselves when we act to help others because our brains exude satisfying dopamine and oxytocin.

However, in the modern world our tolerance has been challenged as the bonds within our own communities have stretched. While individual and regional leaders encouraged observance, it was always local.

Now, through modern technologies, we have a rare ability to create a worldwide movement. The potential for good is enormous. If enough of us subscribe to living compassionately and more sensitively toward others and other forms of life, then we can make a difference.

As the author Dov Seidman explains in his essay, we start at a personal level, then continue at a group level, then reach further still to a global level. Finally, the world starts to change for the better.

In the following pages, the celebrated Professor Johan Rockström scientifically sets out the scale of the threats the Earth faces. A changing atmosphere, species loss and dwindling bio-capacity are among nine significant planetary boundaries he describes. He defines the Earth as "moving out of its Garden of Eden" state to a new, precarious and unpredictable phase.

There is little guarantee we can avoid this fate. However, the United Nation's Sustainable Development Goals and the Paris Climate Agreement, both signed within weeks of each other in 2015, give a guide as to what needs to be achieved. (One essayist, the Unilever CEO Paul Polman, sat on the High Level Panel that helped develop the Goals.) Both agreements are a historic opportunity to create not just a better world, but a remarkable world.

Yet, the process requires resetting our intentions and redesigning our interactions with vision, purpose and also speed. The leading figures grouped together in this journal share the belief that this mission, along with a new sense of global compassion engendered by the Golden Rule can steer the way to a better planet.

It requires a worldwide transformation at times so fundamental that it is difficult to imagine. However, there is a parallel. Most of us know about the incredible metamorphosis of a caterpillar into a butterfly.

The scientific processes that underpin its change

'After a period of ravenous consumption, the caterpillar forms a chrysalis from which it will dissolve itself into an organic stew, where dormant "imaginal cells" hold the vision of the new structure'

are instructive. After a period of ravenous consumption, the caterpillar forms a chrysalis from which it will dissolve itself into an organic stew, where dormant "Imaginal Cells" hold the vision of the new structure.

At first these Imaginal Cells operate independently as single-cell organisms and are attacked by the caterpillar's immune system, which views them as a threat.

But soon these new cells regroup, multiply, and connect with each other. They then form clusters and begin resonating at the same frequency. Finally, they reach a tipping point and consolidate to become a new multi-cell organism – the beautiful butterfly.

Today, with humanity at its own tipping point we face overlapping challenges so great that failure to navigate any one of those challenges (let alone a combination) could threaten our species' survival, as well as other life on Earth.

This is the driving force behind this project: for the visions and ideas put forward by the amazing contributors to this journal to serve as our very own Imaginal Cells.

Our simple project of bringing them together aims to conceive a chrysalis that holds a unified vision of transformation, founded on a simple global principle.

Each essay, or Imaginal Cell, offers a key to transforming an aspect of our small, troubled world, and to realising something almost unimaginably beautiful.

At their collective heart these essays also have the same DNA, a call to treat others as you would like to be treated.

HOME TRUTHS

By Al Gore, Former US Vice President
and Nobel Laureate

WE WILL WIN THIS. The essential mandate in my faith tradition, and in many others is, "Love thy neighbour as thyself." In all traditions, we have been given powerful and eloquent instructions to protect our Mother Earth, our only home. Yet, throughout history we have seen an abundance of confusion between dominion and domination in our treatment of the Earth.

Today, we face an issue of environmental justice on a global scale, but a powerful shift has been taking place around the world. It is clear that we will ultimately prevail through a collective effort to solve the climate crisis. There are three questions that we have to answer about our future:

1. MUST WE CHANGE?
2. CAN WE CHANGE?
3. WILL WE CHANGE?

The answer to the first question necessarily involves some bad news, but the answers to the second two questions involve extremely good news that is surprisingly inspiring!

1. MUST WE CHANGE?

Our reliance on dirty carbon-based fuels during the rise of industrial civilisation brought historic declines in poverty, rising standards of living, and the many blessings associated with our interconnected global economy. Moreover, since we still depend on carbon fuels for approximately 85% of all the energy we use in the world, it is a daunting challenge to shift away from them as quickly as the scientific community believes is necessary.

Nevertheless, we must change. Each day we spew 110m tonnes of man-made, heat-trapping global warming pollution into our atmosphere as if it were an open sewer. Moreover, it is important to note that the sky is not the vast expanse it appears when we gaze up at it from the surface of our planet; rather, it is an extremely thin shell that surrounds the Earth, with a total volume of air so small that its molecular composition can be dramatically altered by the massive injections of gaseous pollution we are constantly injecting into it.

In fact, the cumulative build-up of all that man-made global warming pollution is now raising global air temperatures to levels that are unprecedented since we began measuring and recording temperature with instruments. Indeed, 14 of

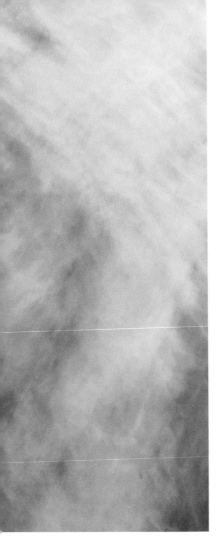

the 15 hottest years ever measured have come in the past 15 years. The hottest of all was 2015; the second hottest was the year before.

Water security is threatened; crop yields are falling from heat stress; land-based plant and animal species are moving poleward at an average rate of 15 feet per day. As many as half of all species may go extinct within the next 85 years. Microbes, including disease-causing viruses like Zika, Dengue and Chinkungunya, are also moving to become endemic in higher latitudes, along with the mosquitos and other "vectors" that spread them.

Significantly, (since 93% of all this extra heat energy is going into the oceans) ocean-based storms are becoming much more powerful and destructive. The heating of the oceans is threatening to disrupt the Gulf Stream and other previously stable ocean currents, and is already dramatically disrupting the hydrological cycle, with huge quantities of additional water vapour rising from the oceans to fuel unprecedented downpours throughout the world. This is causing more extreme floods, including eight "once in a thousand years" floods in the U.S. in just the last ten years. And the rapidly accelerated melting of ice in Greenland and Antarctica is speeding sea-level rise, threatening all low-lying coastal cities, including Miami, New York, Newark, Mumbai, Kolkata and many others.

So, must we change? Yes. Mother Nature and the laws of physics are difficult to ignore.

2. CAN WE CHANGE?

Yes! We're seeing a continuing, sharp, exponential decline in the cost of renewable energy, energy efficiency, batteries and storage – giving nations around the world a historic opportunity to embrace a sustainable future. Indeed, in many parts of the world renewable energy is already cheaper than fossil fuels, and in many developing regions of the world renewable energy is leapfrogging fossil fuels altogether, the same way mobile phones leapfrogged landline phones. And these dramatic cost reductions are not only continuing but accelerating!

Of course, fossil fuels are still subsidised at 40 times the rate of renewable energy sources and the current price of electricity from fossil fuels does not even begin to incorporate the true cost of carbon pollution in our atmosphere. More and more governments and businesses are recognising the need for an accurate assessment of the cost of carbon-based electricity, and some are already adopting a direct or indirect price on carbon. But globally we need to phase out subsidies for carbon-based fuels and put an accurate price on carbon pollution.

The role of the private sector in integrating sustainable capitalism into markets and integrating sustainability into investment strategies is also vital to solving the climate crisis. The flawed metrics of GDP (used since Bretton Woods as the principal compass for the guidance of economic policy) leave

'We are the stewards
of the Earth and
we hold within us
a responsibility
and opportunity to
protect and preserve
our only home for
generations to follow'

us blind to the harmful effects on societies of the rapid rise of inequality in incomes and wealth, the build-up of negative externalities, the neglect of positive externalities, and the unsustainable depreciation of strategically crucial natural resources. These metrics should be enriched with the integration of new measures that allow us to systematically focus on long-term values and sustainability.

3. WILL WE CHANGE?

In December of 2015, 196 nations reached a historic agreement in Paris, against the backdrop of the changes already noted and built on the efforts of governments and businesses to make a significant course change away from "business as usual".

So, will we change? While the answer to this question is up to all of us, the fact is that we are already changing! The only question now is how long will it take to get there?

When any great moral challenge is ultimately resolved into a binary choice between what is right and what is wrong, the outcome is foreordained because of who we are as human beings.

In the great moral challenges of our time – the movement to abolish slavery, the movement to give women the right to vote; the movement to end apartheid, the civil rights movement; and the effort to remove discrimination based on sexual orientation – when people said: "I would not want to be treated that way and I would not want my child treated that way," the outcome became clear.

In the same way, we are the stewards of the Earth and we hold within us a responsibility and opportunity to protect and preserve our only home for generations to follow. But I am optimistic. We are going to prevail. We will win this.

Breaking Bad

Beyond the Nation State: One World Awareness

By Jonathon Porritt, Founder
Director of Forum for the Future

"The world must begin nurturing 'one world' and 'one human family' behaviours based around the Golden Rule", says Forum for the Future founder, Jonathon Porritt.

Illustration by Jacob van Leeuwen

'All of life is interrelated. We are all caught in an inescapable network of mutuality, tied to a single garment of destiny. Whatever affects one directly affects all indirectly.'

- Martin Luther King, Jr.

ON DECEMBER 12TH 2015, the gavel came down on the 21st Conference of the Parties under the United National Framework Convention on Climate Change. The Paris Agreement was done. 196 world leaders returned to their countries celebrating 'a historic deal', a view with which the majority of scientists and NGOs concurred, albeit somewhat less enthusiastically. Not one of them, I imagine, thought the Agreement would be formally ratified within a year. But that's exactly what happened on October 5th 2016, when the required thresholds were passed.

It's been argued that the Paris Agreement is one of the most extraordinary international agreements ever signed. In a world where national self-interest remains as dominant a geopolitical factor as ever (and possibly even more dominant as the EU, where the principles of supranationalism might be said to most ambitiously reside, starts fracturing at the edges), the readiness of so many countries to set aside their own immediate national self-interest was remarkable.

Remarkable – but still inadequate! Climate change is the most comprehensively transboundary challenge of all the challenges facing humankind today. The rationale for countries setting aside a limited amount of immediate national sovereignty is that, in the long run, all countries stand to benefit – even those whose economies are most endangered by the increasingly likely prospect of very significant reserves of coal, oil and gas being left in the ground.

But politicians don't get elected (and autocrats don't go unchallenged) by prioritising the long term over the short term. And the truth of it is that we're going to have to go a great deal further, and a great deal faster, in our decarbonisation journey than anything those world leaders have even started to contemplate. One Parisian swallow (even a ratified swallow!) does not prefigure a gloriously low-carbon summer.

It's been clear to me for a long time that the way in which we respond to the challenge of accelerating climate change will determine not just the future of the nation state but the prospects for humankind as a whole. We can pretty much guarantee that this response will be a terrible muddle (reactive, minimalist, messy etc.), but at the end of that twisty, troubled, turbulent process there are basically only two potential outcomes.

MELTDOWN

If we carry on doing 'too little, too late' at every step of the journey (as we are still doing today) it will indeed prove to be too late. As sea levels rise and weather extremes multiply, existing international treaties will be repudiated, countries will default on existing commitments, nationalism of an increasingly intolerant and xenophobic variety will become the norm, national borders will be strengthened, refugees will be repelled with extreme force. Some countries might weather the storm; most will be crushed. The forward trajectory of human progress will be stopped in its tracks.

BREAKTHROUGH

Now imagine a very different outcome. The unfolding horror story of accelerating climate change compels today's political and wealthy elites (in the face of overwhelming public anger) to complete the transition to a 'net zero emissions' global economy in what today looks like an inconceivably short period of time. Young people start living out, in practice, a One World ethic; the nation state survives, but supranational agreements drive a new kind of solidarity and cooperation. In the face of what has turned out to be a 'real and present danger' of an existential kind, we eventually start living as one human family.

Perhaps understandably, people don't really see it like that today. But using polarised scenarios of this kind may help to awake us to the consequences of what we're doing right now, and where we're headed.

Not least because that 'Breakthrough' scenario won't just fashion itself! In effect, it means recasting our understanding of progress; it demands a different kind of politics, and a radically different approach to education; and it requires reinventing the story that we have of ourselves as a species, through a new cosmology.

The rich vein of literature about this need for a new story (for many, starting with the work of Thomas Berry back in the 1970s) has as yet made relatively little impact on what might be described as 'mainstream world views'. This is both disappointing and very surprising, given that its origins are located firmly in the scientific insights gained from 20th century physics and astronomy. We know now that the interconnectivity between all humans is a physical fact as much as a spiritual revelation or a political aspiration.

'The Earth is not just the environment we live in. We are the Earth, and we are always carrying her within us'

'Everything that exists in the universe came from a common origin. Our ancestry stretches back through all life forms into the stars and back to the beginnings of the primeval fireball. The material of your body and the material of my body are intrinsically related, because they emerged from and are caught up in a single energetic event. This universe is a single, multiform energetic unfolding of matter, mind, intelligence and life. And all of this is new. We are the first generation to live with an empirical view of the origins of the universe. We are the first humans to look into the night sky and see the birth of stars, the birth of galaxies, the birth of the cosmos as a whole. Our future as a species will be forged within this new story of the world.'

There are many definitions of what this new story is all about, most of which (as with that quote above from Brian Swimme. 'The Universe is a Green Dragon') start by locating us firmly in the still-unfolding span of 13.8bn years of the history of the universe. Yet it remains a somewhat slippery notion, hard to pin down, let alone to articulate in

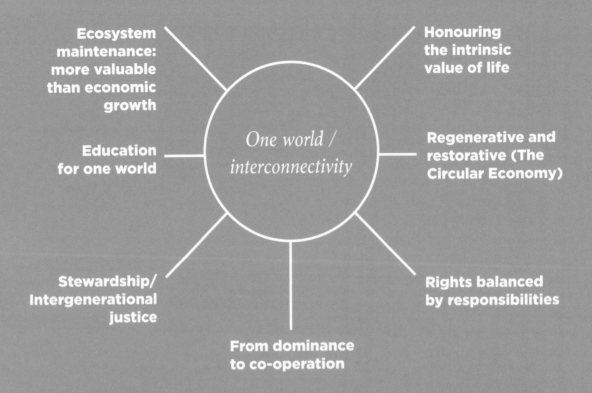

Ecosystem maintenance: more valuable than economic growth

Honouring the intrinsic value of life

Education for one world

One world / interconnectivity

Regenerative and restorative (The Circular Economy)

Stewardship/ Intergenerational justice

Rights balanced by responsibilities

From dominance to co-operation

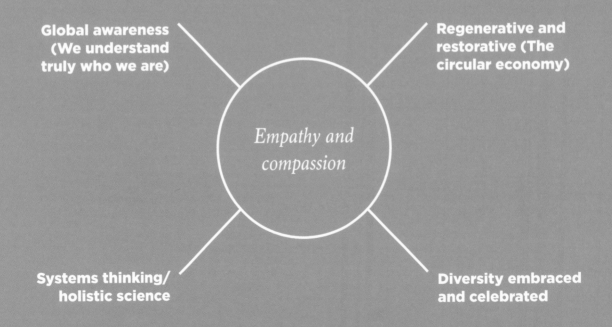

Global awareness (We understand truly who we are)

Regenerative and restorative (The circular economy)

Empathy and compassion

Systems thinking/ holistic science

Diversity embraced and celebrated

such a way as to breathe new life into the efforts of all those seeking a radical overhaul of today's orthodox models of progress.

And that's now critical. I believe it's primarily because we don't have any real sense of what and who we are (as a species and as individuals) that we're so vulnerable both to ideological extremes of every kind, and to the kind of crass, escapist consumerism that stunts people's imagination and kills off any idea of higher purpose. Would we really be living the way we do today if we hadn't been hollowed out by the deceptions and illusions of the 'story' that has come to dominate people's lives since the start of the Industrial Revolution – a story of exploitation, subjugation of the Earth, colonialism, materialism, growth-at-all-costs, and so on?

During a remarkable conference I attended at the Findhorn Foundation in October 2014, on the theme of the 'New Story', a group of us set out to try and capture the essence of what that story is all about. We failed, of course, but we had a lot of fun in the process!

AN UNBROKEN WHOLENESS

Against the backdrop of today's fractured world, driven by heedless competition and the literally impossible dream of permanent exponential growth on a finite planet, the very notion of 'an unbroken wholeness' may well sound fantastical. This makes it all the more important to hold true to a view of human nature informed, first and foremost, by what some have described as our 'compassionate predisposition', our built-in readiness to identify with what someone else is feeling, and then to respond to their feelings with an appropriate emotion.

It's the power of 'as if' – experiencing someone else's joy or suffering as if it were our own, recognising the unifying thread that connects each of us to each other and to all of life on Earth.

Right now, as Europe struggles with the worst humanitarian crisis since the Second World War (horribly torn between the solidarity most feel for the innocent victims of wars in Syria, Iraq, Libya and elsewhere, and a rising fear of what this means

for our existing way of life and identity) it's hard to articulate a compelling vision for any kind of One World philosophy when so many aspects of the nation state (from both a security and a cultural point of view) seem to be at risk.

So what must we do to nurture our 'compassionate predisposition'? In 'The World We Made', writing from the vantage point of 2050 looking back at how we actually succeeded in building a genuinely sustainable world, I speculated that by 2050 we will have succeeded in extending that 'circle of compassion' (to use Albert Schweitzer's phrase) to embrace the whole of life on Earth, and to have refashioned our exploitative and often cruel relationship with other creatures. Moving from 'dominance to cooperation' whilst 'honouring the intrinsic value of life', as represented in that 'Unbroken Wholeness' diagram.

In his extraordinary 'Love Letter to the Earth', Zen Master and peace activist, Thich Nhat Hanh, lays down an even more profound challenge in suggesting that an essential part of becoming 'one human family', free of the constraints of competitive nationalism, is that we will indeed have to change our whole relationship with the Earth:

'The Earth is not just the environment we live in. We are the Earth, and we are always carrying her within us. We are a living, breathing manifestation of this beautiful and generous planet. Knowing this, we can begin to walk differently, and to care for her differently. That is the relationship each of us can have with the Earth. That is the relationship each of us must have with the Earth, if the Earth is to survive, and if we are to survive as well.'

For Buddhists, the simple practices of meditation and mindfulness help breathe life into that kind of renewed relationship with the Earth. Thich Nhat Hanh talks of the need for 'compassionate listening to the Earth' as the fastest and most lasting way of understanding the folly of our current environmental abuses and the need to reconnect quickly to heal both ourselves and the Earth.

I make no apologies for bringing a spiritual dimension into the hard-headed world of the

'Live your life bravely as a citizen of One World so that world may continue to provide a stable and productive home for all people, for all time'

geopolitics of climate change. As the massive surge of interest in the 2015 Papal encyclical about climate change demonstrated, people's religious or faith-based beliefs and values are going to play an extraordinarily important role in shaping both their attitudes and their behaviours over that critical period of time which will lead either to 'Meltdown' or to 'Breakthrough'.

Even in the 'Breakthrough' scenario, the demands on individuals (in terms of the degree to which their values will be tested, and their capacity for tolerance and empathy stretched to the very limit) will be unremitting. Their readiness to live by the Golden Rule will be called into question on a daily basis – and in the midst of any 'Meltdown' impacts on the rule of law, and on the norms of day-to-day decency and civility, one can only assume that the Golden Rule will become the rarest of rare exceptions.

Is that too stark a picture? It may be. But genuine hopefulness for the future depends on never averting our eyes from the prospect of where today's mind-numbingly foolish 'story' about progress, competition and self-destructive sovereignty will take us. As Jeremy Rifkin has mapped out in 'The Empathic Civilization', his extraordinary account of how we are slowly evolving into a species with an ever-greater capacity for empathy, there's something of a race going on here:

'The empathic civilisation is emerging. We are fast extending our empathic embrace to the whole of humanity, and the vast project of life that envelops the project. But our rush to universal empathic connectivity is running up against a rapidly accelerating juggernaut in the form of climate change and the proliferation of weapons of mass destruction. Can we reach biosphere consciousness and global empathy in time to avert planetary collapse?'

I believe we can. *But only if we start nurturing 'one world' and 'one human family' behaviours just as fast as we possibly can, explicitly adding the following rider to the basic Golden Rule: 'Live your life bravely as a citizen of One World so that world may continue to provide a stable and productive home for all people, for all time.'*

HEARTS & MINDS

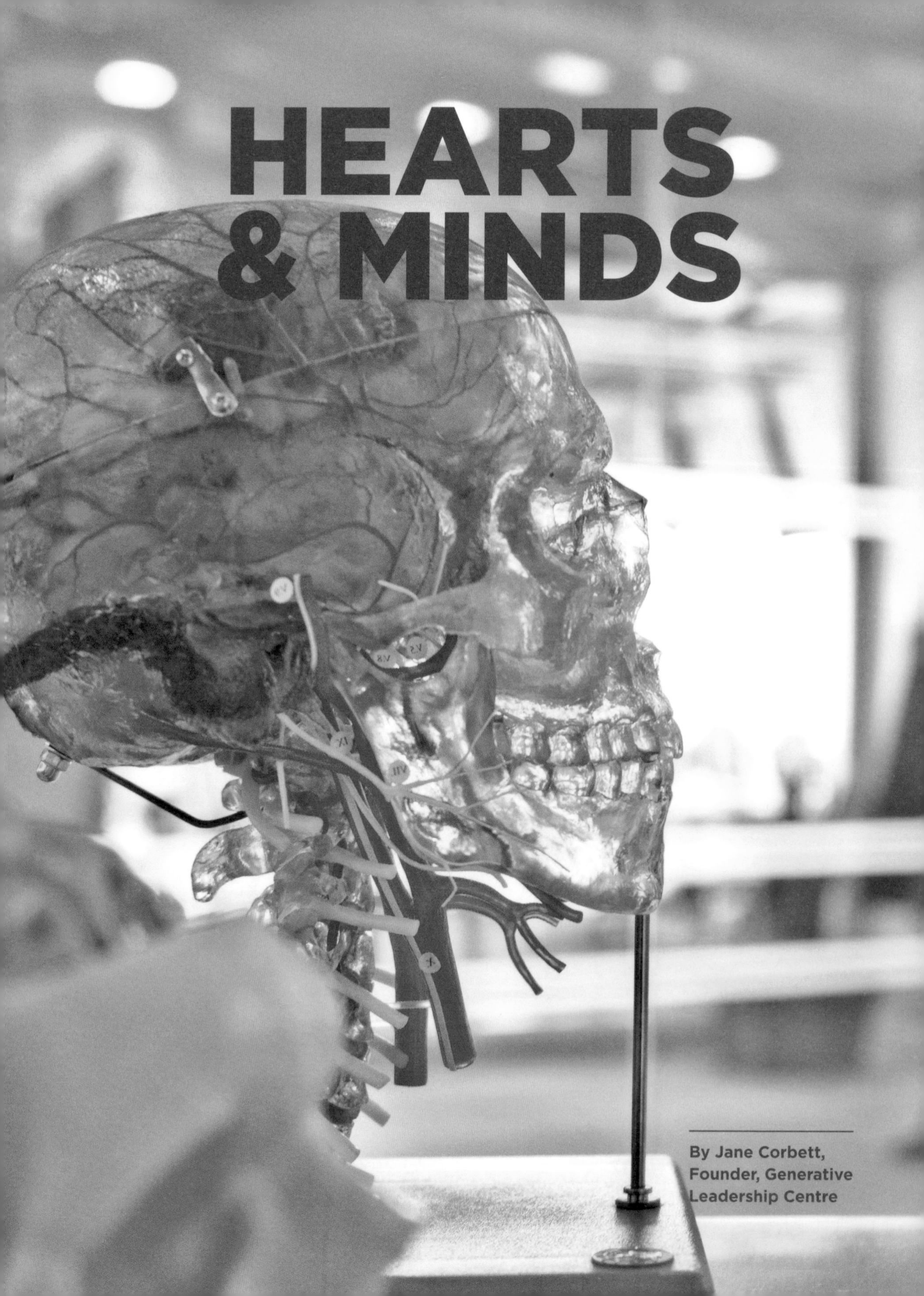

By Jane Corbett,
Founder, Generative
Leadership Centre

The Golden Rule calls on us to treat others as we wish to be treated. Now experts believe a more developed understanding of the heart's rhythms can lead groups to work together in compassionate ways.

CREATING INSPIRED FIELDS OF ACTION. The neurosurgeon James Doty argues that "while survival of the fittest may lead to short-term gain, research shows it is survival of the kindest that leads to the long-term survival of a species".

As a clinical professor of neurosurgery at Stanford University, Professor Doty has demonstrated that compassion has restorative and transformational powers. It does us good and it does others good. There are many implications for how we do business and create partnerships to address urgent societal challenges.

Compassion is wishing that others be free of suffering and having a desire or orientation to alleviate that suffering. It includes the Golden Rule; treating others as you would wish to be treated yourself.

In recent times the science of compassion has begun to suggest that we are wired to practise compassion, with many benefits not just to ourselves, but to others, also meanwhile, intentionally cultivating positive emotional states like compassion can play a very important role in the developmental shifts we need to make to realise our common humanity as we transition to a more sustainable world.

Professor Doty, the founder and director of the Center for Compassion and Altruism Research and Education, points particularly to the role of the heart in making the transformation. "When scientists first started measuring meditation and compassion, it was with Tibetan monks, using electroencephalography (EEG). The instrument of measurement was an EEG electrode cap worn on the head. The monks laughed when they saw the caps. The scientists at first thought that the monks were laughing at the cap because it looked funny, but that was not the case. A monk explained: "everyone knows that compassion isn't in the head. It's in the heart". (Doty 2012)

One of the strongest common threads uniting the views of diverse cultures and spiritual traditions throughout history is the universal regard for the human heart as the source of love, intuition and wisdom. We often speak of the heart colloquially when we say things like, 'in my heart of hearts I know that' or 'my heart's telling me' or 'this goes straight to the heart of things'. The science of compassion and the science of the heart help to validate and expand what we have been experiencing over generations in many human contexts and cultures.

Over 20 years of high quality peer-reviewed science, the likes of the Institute of HeartMath have helped to cast new light and provide evidence on how our hearts work. The heart is a real centre of intelligence; it has its own neuronal networks. It is almost like we have a mini-brain in the heart. Our emotional state is woven into this in very interesting ways. The heart is involved in helping to create emotional experiences, especially positive emotions.

The science of heart-brain communication shows that heart signals affect the brain centres involved in emotion, perception, decision making, reaction times, social awareness and the ability to self-regulate. (McCraty et al 2009)

This research indicates that at the personal

'The Golden Rule calls on us to treat others as we wish to be treated'

level the heart plays a powerful role in facilitating cognitive function, our capacity to work rapidly with intuitive perception, activate foresight, enhance communication and connect at a deeper level with each other in the situations in which we find ourselves.

The HeartMath tools and biofeedback technology trains people to get into heart coherence – generating a stable, sine-wave-like pattern in one's heart rhythms. When the heart rhythm is coherent, the body (including the brain/mind and nervous system) synchronises to the heart's coherent rhythm and we gain greater mental clarity and intuitive discernment, including improving decision-making.

When we experience sincere positive emotions, such as loving, kindness, compassion or gratitude, the heart's rhythm becomes more coherent and harmonious. We can learn to shift into this state of heart coherence to bring the mind and emotions into alignment and have more access to intuitive discernment, often in a very short time (McCraty and Zayas 2014). It takes a little practice to do this on demand, but it gets easier and quicker the more you do it.

With practice, using simple coherence building tools which combine awareness of heart-focused breathing with deliberate cultivation of powerful positive emotional states (like compassion, care or gratitude) can quickly increase coherence at the personal level, with a number of physiological benefits. These tools can also be used to prepare for demanding events, difficult decisions to recover from intensive and stressful work experiences.

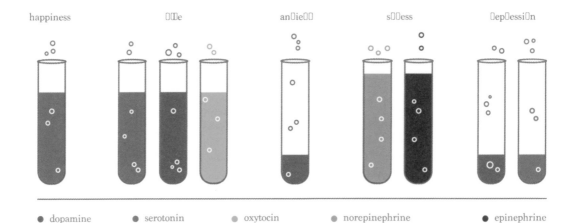

happiness   love   anxiety   stress   depression

● dopamine   ● serotonin   ● oxytocin   ● norepinephrine   ● epinephrine

SOCIAL COHERENCE: ACTIVATING A GROUP FIELD

HeartMath research has also confirmed that when an individual is in heart coherence, the heart radiates a more coherent electromagnetic signal into the environment that can be detected by the nervous systems of other people and animals. At the personal level, we can create a coherent field within and around us. (McCraty 2015)

Practising heart coherence has significant personal benefits. What happens when groups of people are in a coherent state at the same time has been less extensively researched so far, but social coherence is an exciting and fast expanding field of research. In 2015 I coordinated the UK part of the first large HeartMath international study, investigating the synchronisation of Heart Rate Variability in five groups globally (MSS in preparation).

Groups of people who get on well together, or who practise heart coherence together, can become entrained and create a coherent field environment. Collective amplification can occur to create a self-reinforcing field which amplifies and increases beneficial effects. This is a significant finding. It has many implications beyond health and wellbeing for how we connect in work settings and transform performance and outcomes of people working together in tough conditions.

THE BENEFITS OF SOCIAL COHERENCE INCLUDE:

- Increased energy and bonding
- Enhanced communication
- Shorter meeting times
- Creativity and finding solutions to difficult problems
- Seeing things from a new perspective
- Collective intuition
- Faster and more accurate decision-making
- Motivation and momentum to make something purposeful happen
- Enjoying the sense of wellbeing that comes from being part of a coherent group (see McCraty, 2016)

Where there is a high level of trust and connection in a group this kind of heart-based intelligence may happen naturally. But there is a lot we can do to activate this powerfully in groups or teams, especially where training is provided. Recent studies have also suggested that it does not require everyone concerned to be in a coherent state: a critical mass can help to create a field environment which makes it easier for others to move into a coherent state. (Morris 2010)

SOCIAL COHERENCE AND COLLECTIVE INTELLIGENCE

Collective intelligence is the capacity of a group of people to act as if from a unified or single intelligence. Whilst each person still has their unique contribution, these are highly aligned around a common purpose or goal. When groups function in this way it is almost as if the group has moved into 'the zone', or a collective state of flow. Ideas and solutions can be generated much faster and more collaboratively. The sense of connection within the group (and the ability to tune into each other) and it's purpose is deepened, and creativity, foresight, decision making and conflict resolution are enhanced.

This is not just a cognitive state. It is more of an embodied state of leadership or innovation practice. In my facilitation experience it is as if there is a palpable shift in the energy in the room as it becomes more coherent, focused and opens up more possibilities for what can be achieved. It is as if there is an inspired field for action that can form, that keeps groups of people deeply absorbed and connected, however hard the working context. And there is scope for doing this both face-to-face and virtually. This points to new ways we can work more actively with heart-based collective intelligence.

THE POTENTIAL FOR COHERENCE AT THE GLOBAL LEVEL

What kind of effect can this have at a distance, even globally? The Institute of HeartMath has created the Global Coherence Initiative (GCI) as a platform to research and develop global coherence practices. GCI is 'A science based co-creative project to unite people in heart-focused care and intention, to facilitate the shift in global consciousness from instability and discord to balance, cooperate and enduring peace'. (McCraty et al 2012)

A core hypothesis that GCI is researching is that 'large numbers of people creating heart centered states of care, love and compassion will generate a more coherent field environment that can benefit others and help offset the current planetary-wide discord and incoherence'. (HM 2015)

THE CORE GCI HYPOTHESES ARE THAT:

- The Earth's magnetic fields are carriers of biologically relevant information that connect all living systems
- Through our heart rate variability, we are synchronised with the earth's field
- We each have the potential to affect the global information field. Practising compassion and other positive emotional qualities can do so positively

PUTTING COMPASSION AND COHERENCE INTO ACTION AND CREATING INSPIRED FIELDS FOR ACTION GLOBALLY

What might intentionally-created coherent fields make possible in business environments, partnerships or global settings?

A simple thought experiment: what if groups of people leading change, innovating or negotiating on tough issues consciously practice heart coherence tools to create a more coherent field together at the start of critical meetings or events? Even in the midst of very full agendas and complex negotiations, doing this coherence building for a short period of time could transform what becomes

possible. Nor need it include everyone present to have some effect. Consciously creating a coherent field for action first might make a significant difference to driving new initiatives and the collective effort in co-design, co-creation and collaboration on tough challenges.

It could help to facilitate bringing what seemed impossible into the realm of the possible; communicate and connect across diverse agendas; create a bigger and more aligned vision; come up with bold new creative solutions; create roadmaps for turning vision into action or bring the event horizon forward for how soon significant progress can be made.

We could imagine a range of contexts. These could include the re-purposing of existing norms, incentive structures, policies or institutions to address critical 21st century challenges.

DIFFERENT WAYS OF CREATING COHERENT FIELD ENVIRONMENTS

BUILD PERSONAL PRACTICE

It is important that there is at least a core of people cultivating a personal practice. This does not need to include everyone. It can be explicitly working with heart-focused breathing and a positive emotional state like compassion or appreciation. It does not need to include the use of biofeedback technology. For some people it might be deepening an existing mindfulness practice with heartfulness.

GROUP, TEAM OR NETWORK CONTEXTS

To create a more coherent environment, make 'Coherence Practice' an agenda item right at the start, before the main business of the meeting. This creates the field for action. Even 5-10 minutes of shared practice of heart focused breathing, plus cultivating a positive emotional state like compassion or appreciation, can make a difference.

RETREATS FOR SENIOR LEADERS AND INNOVATORS

Build these tools and practices into retreats for people in senior leadership positions who are taking time out to reflect on their experiences with peers, experiment and deepen their practice and see new possibilities for transformational change in organisational or societal contexts.

NEXT GENERATION LEADERSHIP DEVELOPMENT PROGRAMMES

Integrate these practices into leadership development programmes and innovation workshops for next generation leaders and innovators in business, public sector and civil society.

A powerful way to do this is to work with the Theory U approach to developing leadership and innovation capacities. This explicitly works with sensing future possibilities from a place of deep intuition and cultivating the stance of an Open Mind, Open Heart and Open Will. It works systemically and can include going to the edge of a system to see through the eyes of different stakeholders we may not normally come into contact with, and then working with rapid innovation practices. The Presencing Institute at MIT ran a global online course, U.Lab, in 2015 and many participants scattered globally commented on the power of the Global synchronised mindfulness sessions to prepare for rapid innovation.

CREATING MORE COHERENT FIELDS IN GLOBAL, SYSTEMIC AND ORGANISATIONAL CONTEXTS

Such environments could include:

- Davos and related global platforms
- U.N. working sessions
- Business leaders working on repurposing business or operationalising the Sustainable Development Goals
- People leading change and innovation in the financial sector
- Economic systems; facilitating the transition from an ego-economy to an eco-economy
- Partnering beyond the organisation and managing complex webs of relationships
- International negotiations on climate change, biodiversity and pollution
- International platforms engaging leaders across business, government, international organisations, politics and civil society
- Creating new kinds of institutions and international governance

CONCLUSIONS: BUILDING POWERFUL FIELD ENVIRONMENTS FOR TRANSFORMATIVE CHANGE

Both the science of compassion and the science of the heart are generating significant findings for how we re-imagine our shared humanity and the fields of consciousness we interact with. We have the potential to activate new collective capacities of mind and heart and to focus these in different fields of action. This has some exciting implications for the potential shifts that are possible both locally and globally, and how this can be aligned with collective action in the transition to a remarkable world.

Building simple practices into the start of key meetings or events could make a substantial difference to what can be achieved. Even short periods of shared practices could change the way we lead, innovate and co-create, even in very demanding conditions. And it looks like this can have influence in virtual or global settings too. We have untapped capacity to create inspired fields for action.

There is a lot to be explored. Experimenting could speed up and ease some of the tough changes ahead, bringing what seemed impossible into the possible in many institutional, partnership and governance settings.

The Bite

The Bushmaster: one of the world's most poisonous snakes, yet it helps millions control their blood pressure.

By Dr. Thomas Lovejoy, Science Envoy for the US State Department

Extinction rates are up to 1,000 times higher than normal, according to Dr. Thomas Lovejoy, the eminent conservation biologist who is considered to be the 'godfather of biodiversity'. Yet each of Earth's species also holds a vast library of information capable of providing answers to a unique set of biological problems. Here, Dr. Lovejoy warns that we must seek global ecosystem restoration if we hope to leave our extraordinary planet intact for future generations.

NEW YORKERS THINK OF WATER AS SOMETHING THAT COMES OUT OF THE TAP. Like most people, they are blissfully unaware of how a healthy, biologically diverse planet provides for the wellbeing of every individual on a daily basis.

The water that flows through their taps comes directly from the watershed forests of the nearby Catskills, a biodiverse habitat for many marvellous aquatic species, as well as providing very high quality water.

It is one of many ecosystem services that benefit us daily. Elsewhere, in New York State 3tn fruit trees are delicately pollinated. Experts calculate the contribution to the nation's agriculture is $29bn – a job not easily replaced by an army with paint brushes in hand.

Across the world, similar operations play out, largely without us noticing. Our planet continues working as linked biological and physical system. We use the phrase a "Living Planet" as a nice metaphor, but it is a working reality.

In its other roles, biological diversity is also quietly contributing to the advance of the life sciences. Every species constitutes a set of solutions to a set of obscure biological problems, waiting for a Eureka moment.

For the world's longest poisonous snake, the Bushmaster, that moment came when its venom was shown to affect the blood pressure of its victims. That discovery led to the development of ACE inhibitors which hundreds of millions of people now use to control their high blood pressure around the globe.

Meanwhile, a bacteria discovered in a Yellowstone hot spring, Thermos Aquaticus, provided the enzyme that developed PCR (polymerase chain reaction), a chain reaction that multiplies genetic material very quickly. It has revolutionised diagnostic medicine, among many other fields (a personal example was my diagnosis of strep throat within 20 minutes when I had only the most preliminary symptoms). It also enabled the Human Genome Project.

Similar advances are occurring unheralded on a continuing basis. Biodiversity is essentially an enormous library and most of its books have

'Humanity can embrace biodiversity by recognising that human aspiration is best served when embedded in nature'

never been read, even superficially. Instead, it derives from living things, continually exploring and testing new possibilities, while every plant, animal and micro-organism has a pedigree going back 4bn years to the beginning of life on Earth.

The book of Genesis tells us that we were given "dominion" over all this – which gives us apparent license to dominate organisms and ecosystems to the point of wholesale elimination.

However, on closer inspection, the original Hebrew actually means stewardship of the rest of Creation and is thus completely consistent with, and integral to, the Golden Rule.

Today, under our current watch, it is clear that sheer human numbers (7.3bn – or 3 times the population when I was born) are pushing extinction rates to perhaps as much as 1,000 times the norm. Meanwhile, the amount of excess CO_2 in the atmosphere accumulates from centuries of destruction and degradation of modern ecosystems.

But it is also providing us with an extraordinary opportunity, and it is my sincere hope that this pivotal moment will now be the beginning of a fundamental change in our attitude to nature as something to be subdued and eliminated. In its place, humanity can embrace biodiversity by recognising that human aspiration is best served when embedded in nature.

Twice in the history of life on Earth there have been extremely high levels of CO_2 in the atmosphere and both times they were brought down by natural processes to pre-industrial levels. The first was coincident with the arrival of plants on land. The second was with the appearance of modern flowering plants. But they give us a fundamentally important solution to the climate change challenge.

Both are incontrovertible evidence of the power of biology to assist in lowering atmospheric CO_2 concentrations, although they took tens of millions of years.

Today we must consider how to do the same, but faster. Much faster. A planetary scale effort at ecosystem restoration could remove a lot of that carbon from the atmosphere. The Woods Hole Research Centre in Falmouth, Massachusetts has already embarked on a study to show the potential for ecosystems restoration on a global map.

Forests will play a primary role because they are so carbon rich, but so too will the restoration of grasslands, restoring agro-ecosystems so they accumulate rather than leak carbon, producing more fertile soil and restoring coastal wetlands.

The result may avoid as much as 0.5°C temperature change. This restoration effort would mean widespread recognition and embrace of the Living Planet. This would entail profound change in human perception of, and attitude about, the environment, transforming climate change from some hopeless Armageddon-like force to one in which individuals can play important roles even by so simple an act as planting a tree or helping restore a forest or grassland. It can give us hope spiritually, as well as in climate substance.

This kind of vision is congruent with Edward O. Wilson's latest book, 'Half Earth', in which he advocates half of the planet left in nature. It has the potential to stop the Sixth Extinction (which most scientists believe humanity is causing).

If humanity achieves such a transformation it will leave us and future generations with an extraordinary planet on which life has flourished and diversified over billions of years. It will mean our gigantic library of the life sciences will be respected.

Meanwhile, it will not only nourish us, it will be replete with wonder. A Monarch butterfly that has the route of a multi-generation migration programmed in its genes. Beetles which navigate by the stars. Humpbacked whales that beam their songs across entire ocean basins. Giant Amazon waterlilies raising their flower temperatures to attract their pollinators for an overnight stay. The migrations of the Red Knot, a bird that travels from Patagonia to the Arctic tundra in a matter of weeks. Elephants communicating at sound frequencies too low for humans to hear. *The diversity of life is what makes our home planet so very special. What a privilege to be part of this four billion year odyssey.*

HOW ECO SYSTEMS ARE BEING RESTORED

Tijuca National Park, Rio De Janeiro Brazil
One of the largest urban forests in the world.
Hundreds of thousands of seedlings were planted by hand in the 19th and early 20th centuries in an area stripped almost bare by its earlier inhabitants, covering 15 square miles.

This an interesting example from the 19th century of the world's first tropical reforestation project. The Emperor commanded the forest be planted to protect the water supply after the forest had been cut down for sugar and coffee.

The Loess Hills, China
An area the size of France that is named after its soil type that is very prone to erosion.
Centuries of overgrazing and deforestation, and a rapid increase in population, resulted in large areas of desert. But since 1994, a new programme has been trying to increase trees and grass and to convince local people to pen goats to avoid erosion of the silt soils. This is a major reforestation process.

The Adirondacks

The main water source for the Big Apple.

This area of upstate New York was coming under increasing threat from the demands of the city. A multi-billion-dollar filtration plant was proposed, but instead, a far-sighted decision was taken that was considerably cheaper, to restore the watershed. At one tenth the cost of building a new water treatment plant, the 1997 decision was backed by civil engineers who confirmed it was cheaper to treat water that had flowed through forest root systems, which also moderated its temperature.

The American Prairie Reserve, Montana

A new non-profit initiative that hopes to create the largest nature reserve in the United States of 3.5m acres, equal to the size of Connecticut.

The latest purchase in 2016 will turn another 50,000 acres from farmland back to prairie.

THE POLLUTION CENTURY

Bill McDonough has been one of the leading figures designing and defining the circular economy for the past 30 years. Here he reveals why we must move from a pollution century to an ecological one where nothing is wasted, while interpreting the Golden Rule as a call for 'intergenerational compassion' calling on us to "do unto your children as they would have you do unto them.

By William McDonough, Architect, William McDonough + Partners. Co-author, Cradle to Cradle: Remaking the Way We Make Things

OUR HOUSEHOLD IS A MESS.

As 795m people go hungry, a third of our food is wasted: waste that accounts for $940bn in annual economic losses, requiring one quarter of all the water used by agriculture; cropland the size of China; and generating roughly 8% of global greenhouse emissions.

Much of that food itself comes wrapped or boxed in plastic which leaks into the ocean at a rate of 8m tonnes a year – joining the 150m tonnes already floating off our shores.

At current rates, the amount of all ocean-borne plastic will likely outweigh all the fish in the sea by the year 2050. This tide of waste drains our economies, too. Nearly 95% of the material value of all that plastic packaging, roughly $120bn annually, is lost after its first and only use.

While billions enjoy the many benefits of sustained economic growth, the industrial system upon which we depend has disrupted and polluted the Earth.

The past century will be dubbed the 'Pollution Century'. Often, it was said, the solution to pollution was dilution, simply sending our toxins into water to be diluted.

But in dealing with this chaos today, we must do more than simply limit the negative impacts of industry and circulating toxic materials. We must move to a healthy, productive system where growth is valued and there is no such thing as waste.

Trying to be "less bad", to reduce or minimise the impact of industry and commerce, is a common strategy in conventional business. But if your goal is just to reduce your impact or get to zero – zero waste, zero carbon, zero emissions, you are only defining what you don't want, not asking what you might create "for the benefit of all".

Let's face it, we are all carbon-based life-forms. If the goal is only to use 20% less carbon, you might as well cut your own leg off.

Instead, why not strive to have a positive, beneficial impact on the planet with a virtuous economy, rather than being less bad within a destructive system?

Good design allows us to do that by following the laws of nature. Rather than limit growth, we can grow in ways that replenish, restore and nourish the world.

There are many things we all want to grow. Education, health, opportunity, more clean water, fresh air, healthy food and shared prosperity. Whatever positive aspiration we might pursue, design gives us the capacity to cultivate good, regenerative growth: making the world better because we are here.

The circular economy doesn't simply minimise waste: it eliminates the very concept of waste and establishes cycles of endless resourcefulness.

The economic benefits are substantial. A 2013 study by McKinsey & Company estimated that a transition to the circular economy in the European Union would provide $1tn in annual savings by 2025 and create 100,000 jobs within five years.

Recently, I have been working on a project to replace steel and wood with more modest items to aid those in poorer societies, by considering how to make building materials from disused plastic.

We are in the middle of reinforcing discarded plastics to make them ultra stable, strong and durable, while working with four companies across Brazil, Chile, Columbia and Mexico.

I have also spent considerable time studying the trash heaps of the world and looking how to mine them for useful effect. This approach is combined with looking at what is discarded, so that we can get signals for how to redesign what goes to waste in the first place. Over the next few decades I can envisage a situation where we remove the antimony from plastic bottles made of polyethylene terephthalate (known as PET).

Could we even reach a situation where plastic is reclaimed for its value? To evaluate this statement, we must ask ourselves if the outcome could see reclaimed plastics worth more than oil and methane?

Certainly the rise of solar energy, which is now being produced more cheaply than gas, is a prime example of how an embryonic industry can develop. Solar has become commoditised in the past decade after the Germans built a market for it and the Chinese worked to commercialise it.

So we could certainly see the same happening with polymers, which may be seen as high value materials if they can be designed with that purpose in mind.

'THE GOLDEN RULE IS A CALL FOR 'INTERGENERATIONAL COMPASSION' CALLING ON US TO "DO UNTO YOUR CHILDREN AS THEY WOULD HAVE YOU DO UNTO THEM"'

The next century must be the 'Ecological Century'. We can ask these design questions that inspire our creativity and generate tremendous value. How can this project make a positive difference in the life of the local community? How might it create habitats, nourish the landscape, and restore biodiversity? How much shared prosperity can we grow? That is how we wage peace through commerce.

The German chemist Michael Braungart and I first posited this values-based design framework to chart a path of continuous improvement with regenerative, circular flows of safe, valuable materials, energy, water and social benefit in 'Cradle to Cradle: Remaking the Way We Make Things' (2002).

Our first principle, 'insist on the right of humanity and nature to exist in a healthy, diverse and sustainable condition', declared our intention to build relationships (whether between buildings and places, or companies and the sources of their wealth) that support the well-being of all living things. Among the other key principles was that design is the first signal of human intention.

Our work was modelled on the nutrient flows of natural systems. In nature, the processes of every organism contribute to the health of the whole. One organism's "waste" becomes food for another, and the fundamental nutrients that support life flow perpetually in regenerative cycles of birth, decay and rebirth: everything is food.

This shows products can be conceived as biological nutrients, products of the biosphere, which are designed to be returned to the earth after use: rebuilding the soil and feeding new growth; or as technical nutrients, products of the technosphere, designed to flow in continuous cycles of use, recovery, and re-manufacture, feeding the creative work of industry.

This is far superior to conventional forms of recycling, which typically downgrade and mix incompatible materials and uses, putting materials in the wrong hands or in the wrong place.

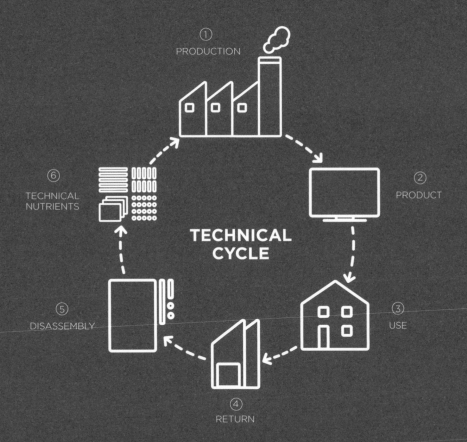

① PRODUCTION

② PRODUCT

③ USE

④ RETURN

⑤ DISASSEMBLY

⑥ TECHNICAL NUTRIENTS

TECHNICAL CYCLE

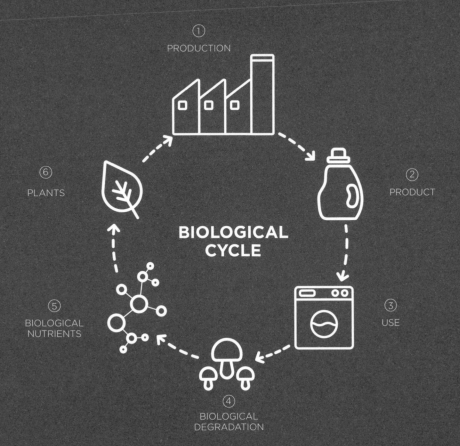

① PRODUCTION

② PRODUCT

③ USE

④ BIOLOGICAL DEGRADATION

⑤ BIOLOGICAL NUTRIENTS

⑥ PLANTS

BIOLOGICAL CYCLE

Illustration by James Fentiman

On the manufacturing side, circular strategies allow intelligent companies to put the 're' back into resources sustaining long-term growth, while the products of circular economies fulfil their purpose by providing access to a service. Rather than buying a car, for example, one may choose to buy access to mobility. People can choose products of service for their qualities and performance, while their makers can "retain ownership" of materials so that the product's embedded quality can be easily recovered and redeployed.

The transition is well underway, worldwide and on multiple scales. Shaw Industries, the world's largest carpet manufacturer, guarantees the recovery of its Cradle to Cradle Certified carpet tiles, printing a 1-800 number on the back of each tile to facilitate its return.

Having made its product with materials that are healthy and safe, and that retain their value for infinite cycles of use, Shaw gladly answers every call and uses recovered tiles as raw materials for the next generation of carpet, saving $4m annually on water and energy costs in the process. Currently these products designed for the circular economy account for $2.4bn of Shaw's $4bn annual total sales. Desso, a European carpet maker, has adopted the same strategy.

These early adopters carry unique burdens; true for any major transformation. But an emerging circular economy depends upon well-organised collaboration, extending throughout supply chains and across national borders, realising the opportunity of cooperation at a depth and on a scale rarely seen in world affairs... and it is happening.

I have the privilege of working closely with the China Association of the Circular Economy, which is developing China's next 5-year plan with new government ministers and hundreds of the nation's largest companies. In Europe, the Netherlands recently established a 3.5km^2 National Hub for the Circular Economy adjacent to the Amsterdam Airport Schipol, while the UK-based Ellen MacArthur Foundation and the World Economic Forum have made a significant investment in raising awareness of the circular economy.

These networks represent what the American Founding Fathers like Benjamin Franklin called "systems of public virtue." Franklin believed people could be encouraged to do things "for the Benefit of Mankind." As the philosopher Lewis Hyde pointed out, he did not consider himself (or most people) to be especially virtuous, however he thought principles could be and they could be enlisted to create structures or institutions (including markets) through which individuals could contribute to the common good. As Hyde writes, these are systems in which the good is pronounced "ahead of time."

Where the circular economy is being adopted, systems of public virtue are organised by establishing values-based platforms for innovative, cooperative work and offering individuals, companies, and institutions from many walks of life a valuable opportunity to realise their goals and aspirations, while contributing to the common wealth.

The five principles of becoming beneficial by design, as described by the Cradle to Cradle Certified Products Program, are: material health (products that can safely return to nature or industry in biological or technical cycles), material re-utilisation, clean energy, water stewardship, and social fairness.

Leading companies from nearly every sector of the global economy and enterprises with trillions of dollars in revenue, as well as thousands of start-ups, are working with these ideas every day.

We're building factories that can not only make these products, but operate in concert with natural systems, making use of the sun, the landscape, and natural flows of fresh air and water to cycle nutrients, power operations, grow food, and create productive, restorative workplaces.

The solar energy company Sun Power is building photovoltaic power fields that perform like working farms – I call them "Solar Orchards". Arrays of solar panels elevated above the ground become like trees, shading the earth and providing habitat for native grasses, which capture water, nitrogen and carbon, building soil health, and provide food for grazing sheep, which in turn provide wool. By design, a solar power plant's relationship to its surroundings creates an abundance of benefits: electricity, habitat, soil restoration, water conservation, wool products, manufacturing and farming jobs, fresh vegetables, fibre, protein, and more.

Places such as these offer an inspiring model for 21st century industry. They show that community and company prosperity are closely entwined and that we all benefit when we support each other, future generations, and the natural world.

Having been involved for most of my life in rendering visible the possibilities of good design in projects all over the world, I am hopeful that we can cultivate our interest in the fortune of others even further, to include not just our friends and peers, but other species and future generations.

To do so, we humbly return to our design values, and as we think about them through the lens of compassion, we see that the Golden Rule is not just for now and not just for us; not just for some children and not just for some species; but is a call to intergenerational compassion which might suggest, "do unto your children as they would have you do unto them"– words implicit in the Cradle to Cradle: How do we love all of the children, of all species, for all time?

As a designer, I believe that is the question of our time. One which will require cycles of endless compassion and creativity, as well as cycles of endless resourcefulness. Cultivating abundance, generosity, and hope, rather than fear, limits, and greed. We will wage peace with commerce, reframing its fundamental question from, "How much can I get for how little I give?" to "How much can we give for all we get?"

TROUBLED WATERS

By Claire Nouvian, Founder and Chair of conservation
organisation BLOOM and Frédéric Le Manach

WE HAVE
DECLARED WAR
ON THE OCEAN

Smashed together. Skinned. Swim bladders protruding, broken jaws, bulging eyes. Thousands of fish compressed in a gigantic net are brought onboard after hours of trawling the seafloor, breaking all forms of life that may have taken hundreds or thousands of years to grow. This huge mass of suffocating, dismantled fish is then swallowed down the well, towards a conveyor belt. On deck, a few leftover gaping fish are trodden on, kicked aside or thrown overboard as waste.

This could be a vision from Dante's Inferno or a Bosch painting, but this is what happens every day at sea on industrial bottom trawl fishing boats.

When seen for the first time, the scene is hard to believe, heart–wrenching, simply revolting. Dozens of species are caught but only a few are of commercial interest. The ones that are not tasty enough, or too bony by market standards, are thrown back in the water, dying or already dead. Those of commercial interest are often too damaged to be presented whole to customers so they are filleted.

This vision of hell is not limited to one particular fishery, like the deep-sea trawling industry. It is widespread. In 2014, Greenpeace exposed the behaviour of tropical tuna fisheries using fishing aggregating devices (so called "FADs"). Their video unveiled a kilometre-long net that traps not only an entire school of tuna, but many other species: mako, silky and whale sharks; sea turtles, marlin, swordfish and dolphinfish. All these unwanted species are separated from tuna and left dying on deck. Once the 'interesting' fish are put into brine, the others are disposed like garbage. In technical terms, they're "by-catch" and soon become "discards".

This is reminiscent of what Charles Patterson described in his book 'Eternal Treblinka' quoting Upton Sinclair's public outcry when faced with the brutality of slaughterhouses. In 1906, Sinclair's book described the unbearable reality of mass killings. As German philosopher Theodor W. Adorno wrote: "Auschwitz begins wherever someone looks at a slaughterhouse and thinks: they're only animals".

Did Sinclair's descriptions lead to a global rejection of what it took to have sausages for breakfast daily? While the young writer was aiming for "the public's heart", all his precious testimony did was "hit it in the stomach", to his despair.

Has our empathy evolved for the condition of animals? Every year, well over 50bn terrestrial animals are killed for human consumption, often in intolerable conditions. If we fail to show interest, let alone compassion for mammals, our chance to feel for fish is slim.

As a result, instead of incorporating higher environmental, well-being and quality standards for its fishing practices, Europe is now quickly endorsing the unthinkable: "pulse fishing", i.e. the latest, most refined technological development consisting of electrocuting fish before collecting them. It is argued that this fishing technique is more efficient and less

fuel intensive than bottom trawling. At what price?
The electric current, which is sent through electrodes
on a frame that trawls the seafloor, convulses marine
organisms of all kinds. Animals with a backbone often
have their spine broken. Others, knocked out for the
best, burnt and dead for the worst, are forced out of
the sediment, where they get collected by the trawl net.

WHAT'S WRONG WITH OUR
FISHING INDUSTRY?

In all instances – bottom trawling, tuna purse-
seining, pulse fishing, etc – the problem is the
scale of the industry. "We have declared war on
fish" summarised Professor Daniel Pauly from the
University of British Columbia. We have applied
military technology to chase fish (GPS, sonars, radars
etc.) and have won the war a long time ago already.
Our technological capacities have proven to be no
match for the inherent biological vulnerability of
marine life. The productivity objectives set forth
by demanding business plans have led to the great
demise of the last and biggest wild biomass on Earth.
The clock is ticking: in 30 minutes, the net must be
cleaned up, sorted out and ready to be redeployed.

'THE BOTTOM LINE, AND GOLDEN RULE, IS THAT IT IS NOT POSSIBLE TO DESTROY NATURE AND EXPLOIT IT ON AN INDUSTRIAL SCALE WITHOUT TAKING A HIT'

There's no time to care about that gaping shark or injured turtle. So we become indifferent and accept that these are casualties and that there is no way around it.

Fish have become a commodity and our appetite made us lose sight of the fact that fish are a fragile resource. Once depicted as bountiful, the ocean is now emptying: we have been losing 1.2m tonnes of wild fish catch every year since 1996. As a result, in 2016, the Food and Agriculture Organisation of the United Nations published the following alarming figures: almost a third of all fish stocks are overexploited; another half is fully exploited and could not stand any more pressure. One quarter of the global fish catch is reduced into fishmeal and fish oil to feed farmed salmon, pigs and poultry.

Not only do marine life and environments get abused and brutalised, so do humans. Numerous stories of slavery and unethical practices in the fishing industry have been revealed by investigative journalists.

The bottom line, and Golden Rule, is that it is not possible to destroy nature and exploit it on an industrial scale without taking a hit. Not only a moral hit for human nature, but a serious blow to the long-term productivity of ecosystems and the diversity of species.

For decades, governments have funded destructive practices with public money. For fisheries, this short-sightedness has resulted in the destruction of coastal communities, the erosion of biodiversity and marine habitats, and the overexploitation of most fish stocks. We need to reverse this trend and this can only be achieved by redirecting public funds towards more virtuous practices and the restructuring of coastal communities. By doing so, more jobs would be created and nature's surplus could be harvested more respectfully and rationally. Fish would still be killed, of course, but the ocean would not have to be bulldozed to dust every time we go fishing.

EMPATHY IS THE SOLUTION

In a remarkable landmark book, Simon Baron-Cohen explains
how empathy has been taken for granted and largely overlooked,
despite it being "one of the most valuable resources in our world".
Empathy is effective in resolving all conflicts, but unlike the arms
industry that costs trillions of dollars, this "universal solvent" which
dissolves any problem is free.

'EMPATHY HAS BEEN TAKEN FOR GRANTED AND LARGELY OVERLOOKED. EMPATHY IS EFFECTIVE IN RESOLVING ALL CONFLICTS'

THE WOOD
FOR THE TREES

By David Mayer de Rothschild, Chief
Curiosity Officer of Lost Explorer

We can regain our sense of purpose by rediscovering that Nature is us and we are Nature.

'It's time to pay Nature some of the debt we owe it'

THE GREEN MOVEMENT HAS FOCUSED TOO MUCH ON CLIMATE CHANGE. People devote a lot of large and lofty talk to Nature. It is still the deficit decor of our fantasies and paradises – just take a quick glance at the nearest advert. Yet millions of people are losing their relationship with it at a young age. They don't have the empathy for it.

The problem is that somewhere along the way we've forgotten that Nature is more than climate change, a concept that has obstinately taken over our entire perception of the outside world.

We've mono-cropped its brilliance and complex diversity into a series of catchphrases originating from the two emotionless and unerring pillars, 'Energy and Carbon,' words that do nothing more than reflect our consumer lifestyles.

As much as it pains me to say it, the Green movement bears a lot of responsibility for this. It has become disparate and factionalised, while obsessively quantifying and observing its disappearance, measuring the rate of its elimination.

Green groups themselves are split into separate organisations representing oceans, wildlife, birds, insects, national parks; often failing to collaborate together because they might lose funding. Together they reduce Nature to abstract terminology like 'environment',

'carbon emissions' and 'climate change', but the message fails to hit its mark.

The human race tells itself it wants to love Nature, but I don't know that we do. If you review the past couple of hundred years, you'll see an odd trend emerging. Even as we've become more and more emphatic in our praise for Nature, we've gone about destroying her with feverish intensity.

Every minute of every day we're doing all sorts of colossally awful things to the planet: sawing down thousands of acres of tropical rainforest, dumping tens of thousands of tonnes of plastic into our oceans, and pumping noxious chemicals into the atmosphere with such coordinated zeal that you'd think it was our divine function.

Why would we ever act like this? We know that this is the only planet we've got and that living within our ecological limits is no longer a negotiable matter. We also know in our guts that Nature is good. I've never met a person who has a problem with it. I don't believe paper company workers hate trees or that oil executives despise glaciers. So why do we act as we do?

So perhaps it's time to pay Nature some of the debt we owe it. Often it is the resources that are paid for that people take care of, while those that can be used for free are taken for granted. But our world is not an extra or an offset. Globally, $580bn a year is spent on marketing. The auto industry alone spends around $44bn a year and is one of the biggest users of Nature in its advertising, in naming and marketing.

But what if just 1% of that spend were directed back to restoring Nature's capital? Any time it is used to sell a brand or advertise a product, companies should pay a royalty that pays Nature back by protecting the talent, beauty and appeal it offers. Some of the largest companies in the world are exploiting our landscape but not contributing anything back. There are a few people and companies who control the majority of resources of the Earth. So, you have to ask, if they make their money from damaging nature, should they not have a responsibility for putting something back to it too?

When it comes to trying to integrate back into Nature, none of us is perfect, especially myself. Often I find myself

higher awareness than ever when it comes to climate messaging. But even with the results of a changing planet unfolding in front of our eyes, when it comes to closing the gap on matching our awareness to meaningful action, we are losing. The language we use to speak of the world and its creatures, including ourselves, has gained a certain expertish pomp, but has lost much of its power to convey any respect, care or devotion toward it. As a result, we've lost a lot of genuinely concerned people and are losing the stories to inspire action.

We have to feel that we love the thing we are trying to protect and that it is relevant on a very basic

falling into the same traps that I am trying to educate people about. It's these lessons and reality checks that leave me more certain than ever that having the ability as an individual to be more open, honest, realistic, and humble about the challenges we face might also be one of the greatest tools for change.

In today's world, there may be a

level. We need an understanding that everything is interconnected and interdependent: businesses, economies, societies and ecologies, me and you. There are no easy answers, no final destination, and no one-size-fits-all solutions, but the interconnectivity is our most promising hope for revitalising it.

It is our Golden Rule. The most vital step of that journey is getting smarter about the way we think, about problem-solving and working together.

It's because of this inter-connectedness that I am calling on world leaders, environmentalists, innovators, artists and global citizens to unite in giving Nature a voice at the United Nations. To reinvigorate and refocus broad environmental awareness at the UN in order to fill a dangerous gap that has opened in lieu of the global climate change emergency.

We need a new global solidarity that pressures world leaders to acknowledge and act on a broad spectrum of environmental issues. The stepping-stone for undertaking this would be to push for the UN's 1982 World Charter for Nature to be updated and retabled at the next General Assembly in 2017.

Reissuing this Charter is the first step toward that solidarity and the greater aim of securing the legitimacy and rights for Nature that are afforded to every member of the UN General Assembly.

It will bring together the greatest hearts and minds of our times to serve as the voice for Nature, speaking on its behalf to ensure Nature's interests are being represented and reflected in how we are shaping the future of our world.

By using and updating the World Charter for Nature, we have the perfect framework to extend the conversation beyond the current one concerning climate change, to one that incorporates the ongoing degradation and vulnerability of our natural world as a whole and stopping this degradation so that people and planet can live in harmony for millions of years to come.

We have externalised ourselves from the web of life and ultimately we need to reintegrate ourselves back in. Finding that sense of purpose will come from recognising that Nature is us and we are Nature.

GREEN MONEY

BALANCING NATURE'S BANK ACCOUNT

By Peter Bakker, President and CEO, World
Business Council For Sustainable Development

***If you don't put a value on something,
people will use it without limit***

EVERY HUMAN DEPENDS ON NATURE, just as every human
has an impact on nature. Every business depends on nature, just
as every business has an impact on nature. Every country depends
on nature, just as every country has an impact on nature.

This is not breaking news. Climate change is happening
and science is indisputably clear about the fact that human
activity is driving these changes.

Weather patterns are visibly changing in all parts of the
world, bringing hotter summers; more severe storms and tornados;
droughts driving nomad populations out of their own areas; floods
disrupting cities, supply chains and ordinary people's homes.
Water stress is now a real phenomenon in cities around the world.
The extinction rate of species in the animal and plant population
is higher than it has ever been. Anyone who has visited the
intricate beauty of rainforests in South America will be unable
to comprehend that since 1990, 129m hectares of all forests on
Earth (an area as large as South Africa, according to the Food and
Agriculture Organisation of the United Nations (FAO)) have been
destroyed by humans.

It is not just the environment that is screaming at us.
More than 800m people are going to bed hungry every night.
Every six seconds a child dies from hunger related causes, and yet
we know we lose or waste more than a third of the food our planet
provides us. At the other end of the scale, 2015 was the first year
in which the number of obese people on our planet surpassed the
number of malnourished. This will have devastating impacts on
human health.

All of these examples are symptoms of a system that
is reaching its limits – a system that has no self-correcting
mechanism. A system that is broken.

All these symptoms are telling us that unless we all
radically transform the way we eat, move and live, the clash
with nature will intensify with little doubt about who will win.
*Everything humans do depends on nature, but human impacts are now
becoming so big that Nature no longer can or will deliver.*

A COURSE CORRECTION

One of the most compelling concepts to explain the growing tension between humans and Nature is "Earth Overshoot Day". Each year, The Global Footprint Network calculates the date on which the total consumption of resources by all human activities equals what the planet is able to renew in one year. As the population globally grows, and as more people are being lifted out of poverty and into the middle classes, that date strikes earlier in the year.

In 2015, Earth Overshoot Day was calculated to be on 13th August 2015. This means that from 14th August until the end of the year the Planet's reserves were being consumed – further limiting its ability to deliver the needs of all people.

If this is too abstract a notion, simply compare this to your own personal bank account. The interest earned by your capital reserve would pay for all of your activities until 13th August. Thereafter, each day you would be eating into your own sum of money, reducing the level of interest that would pay for all costs next year. Not a wise financial strategy to live one's life. Not something we should do to Nature either.

For a world that is less than 50 years old, it is remarkable how tired 'sustainability' can feel at times. Many people associate it with 'tree-huggers' and 'naysayers'; good at pointing out the symptoms, at times at risk of spreading doom and gloom, best of intentions, full of good will, but no real impact. Much talk but little action. What the movement needs now to capitalise on the Paris Agreement and the adoption of the Sustainable Development Goals is a new mindset aimed at scaling up the solutions. What the movement needs is to stop fighting the symptoms and start changing the system. What we need is nothing short of a revolution in our economics.

Three elements will create the scale to make humans bring their relationship with nature back in balance: innovation, collaboration and redefining valuation.

1 INNOVATION will make us find pathways and solutions that reduce the impacts and maximise the opportunities in the way we live, produce and consume. We're making progress but innovation efforts need to accelerate and scale up. Electric vehicles on renewable energy are better than the gas-guzzlers that we use today. Concepts like the circular economy, where we use, re-use and recycle will lower the demand on Earth's resources. Smarter diets will provide the nutritional values we need to live healthily, while reducing the footprint to produce and distribute food to all in a fair way.

2 COLLABORATION is the only way we will be able to implement the solutions at scale and speed. Businesses must work together within sectors and value chains to identify the solutions. Governments, cities and businesses must work together to implement the solutions. Everything must be based on science to ensure we are addressing the challenges identified in the Planetary Boundary Framework.

3 REDEFINING VALUE is changing the way we value performance and which economic incentives we integrate in our decision-making. At the core of today's economic system we only value financial capital and exclude many elements on which we depend for those future cash flows to materialise. These excluded elements are therefore appropriately called the 'externalities'.

TOWARDS INTEGRATED CAPITALISM

In a 2015 FAO study, Trucost calculated that the externalities associated with crop and livestock production alone were $2.96tn, 146% of their production value. Or, in other words, if Nature would send us a bill for all the services she provides (like water or pollination) and we account for the damages firms do (for instance in greenhouse gas emissions, air, land and water pollution or with waste) then the food we produce would cost almost 2.5 times what we currently account for. But Nature does not send invoices and therefore these "externalities" are what we call non-financial, or non-cash, items.

The problem is that the current mainstream definition of value is based solely on the notion of future cash flows, which is clearly too limiting a view of value in the context of the massive non-cash externalities. This view of value may have served society well in a world that seemed to have limitless resources and no planetary or social boundaries, but the symptoms above illustrate clearly that such a world no longer exists.

'EVERYTHING HUMANS DO DEPENDS ON NATURE, BUT HUMAN IMPACTS ARE NOW BECOMING SO BIG THAT NATURE NO LONGER CAN OR WILL DELIVER'

Illustration by James Fentiman

Our task now is to find a way to integrate the externalities in our decision-making. In simple terms, we must begin to value Nature.

Simply ask yourself: if companies can deplete natural resources and pollute the atmosphere without paying for it, why would they invest in cleaner technology? If the information on, and price of, food products don't reflect the related health costs related to dietary impacts, what are the incentives to change the recipes? What incentives are there for a government to change its policies if the measure for political success (i.e. GDP) does not include any of the detrimental impacts these policies may have on their country's natural resources?

Fixing the broken economic system therefore means moving from Financial Capitalism to Integrated Capitalism. Plans for new systems, like the Natural Capital Protocol, can calculate the externalities and how companies should measure and manage them.

Four years ago people were incredibly sceptical about this issue, but now 38 diverse organisations have worked together to develop the Natural Capital Protocol. Its launch in the World Conservation Congress led to widespread engagement with the subject.

The next step is to make the Protocol align with reporting frameworks like the Global Reporting Initiative, an international independent reporting standards organisation that has 9,000 companies worldwide reporting on their non-financial impacts. Thereafter, the next step

'THE PROBLEM IS THAT THE CURRENT MAINSTREAM DEFINITION OF VALUE IS BASED SOLELY ON THE NOTION OF FUTURE CASH FLOWS'

will be to integrate the sustainability indicators into mainstream corporate reporting standards.

One company that has pushed this way of management furthest is Kering, the French luxury goods group that owns Gucci, Dior and Puma. Kering created Environmental Profit and Loss (EP&L) accounting and now applies it for management decision making in all its subsidiaries. The firm asked to what extent could it put a price on water, land use and pollution? It turned out that these environmental costs were almost half of their traditional financial profit. This subsequently led them to use environmental cost accounting to enable better product and production decision-making, reducing the environmental damage and improving their EP&L.

In Integrated Capitalism, the value is not limited to "future cash flows", but is based on integrating the externalities to calculate the returns on Financial, Social and Natural Capital. This takes the concept of the triple bottom line of People, Planet and Profit to another level by making it more robust, systematic and mainstream.

In a world that is dominated by money, the forces making decisions based on profit are so much stronger than those driving the people or planet elements. This means that only in excessive situations or niches of the markets will the attention on the latter two change decisions materially.

In Integrated Capitalism, the risk-management, decision-making, governance, disclosures and (eventually) capital allocations will be based on Financial, Social and Natural capital. The objective can no longer be to only maximise returns on Financial capital. Instead, we must focus on optimising the balance and longevity of returns on all three capitals and on being transparent about the trade-offs that must inevitably be made between them.

For this transformation of our economic system a whole new mindset and toolkit is required. On the left side of our brain, we must learn to value Nature, or in economic terms we must pay for the externalities and learn to think of the services that Nature provides as capital. Our collective objective must be to preserve or maximise that capital for the long-term.

To make this happen, a whole host of initiatives are being developed around the world – ranging from the Natural Capital Protocol, Integrated Reporting Framework, Sustainable Accounting Standards and Carbon Pricing Leadership Coalition, through to the Taskforce on Climate-related Financial Disclosures. All of these are pieces of the toolkit needed to make the new system measure and integrate the value of Nature in decision-making and reporting. It is in this way, when faced with a multitude of global threats, that we may discover that it is accountants who may be able to save the world.

On the right side of our brain, the Golden Rule can play a crucial role. When asked for the meaning of sustainability, most people will come up with an answer that it is about leaving the world for our children and grandchildren in a better place than we found it ourselves. This parent-child notion itself contains much of the meaning of the Golden Rule. It is no coincidence that we often refer to Nature as "Mother Nature". With tensions rising, it would be good to apply the Golden Rule to her.

Let's all do to Mother Nature what we want done to our children, our grandchildren and ourselves.

Illustrations by Ester Vilaplana

THE REFUSE REFUSAL

By Tom Szaky, CEO and
Founder TerraCycle

TerraCycle CEO Tom Szaky warns that what we do to our world ultimately comes back to us - in our food, in our water, and in our air.

95% OF EVERYTHING WE MAKE BECOMES WASTE AFTER A SINGLE USE. Today, more than 150 years after the light bulb was invented, an average modern incandescent bulb lasts 750 hours.

Yet in Livermore, California, an incandescent light bulb has been burning non-stop for 110 years. Why? Interestingly, just over ninety years ago the world's major light bulb manufacturers got together in Geneva and created a cartel called Phoebus to reduce the life of a light bulb. By making the filaments more fragile than they needed to be, bulbs would burn out more quickly. The industry grew and shareholders rejoiced.

However before 1924, the average bulb lasted about 2,500 hours. Within a decade following the cartel meeting, it was at 1,500 hours. Since then it has declined to today's 750 hours.

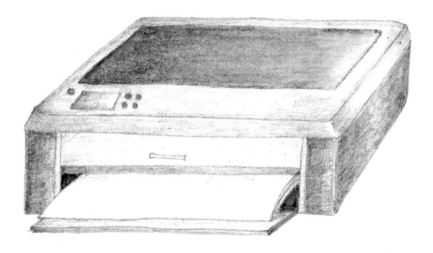

As incredible as this sounds, it is a pattern that has echoed across the past century. Whether it's an EPROM chip that purposefully disables many inkjet printers after 20,000 pages printed, to General Motor's alleged cancelling of the original electric car (the EV1) due to the lack of mechanical servicing it would need in the future.

In the name of profit, instead of designing away problems we have mastered the art of doing the inverse.

In recent months, Apple released the iPhone 7 and eliminated the headphone jack. Was it an effort at making design improvements? Most likely. But it has also been a phenomenally profitable thing to do, as iPhone 7 users are given an adaptor and a wired set, but must now acquire their own more expensive wireless headphones. It's therefore hard to believe the design improvement was not also economically motivated. Another consequence of this iPhone evolution is that now, millions of perfectly functional headphones that require jacks, will become waste.

Just another unfortunate impact of our industrial world wearing principally short-term profit-driven lenses, is that globally 95% of what humans produce becomes waste after a single use. That's right – we only recycle about 5% of all the waste we produce and some studies show that 25% of the balance ends up in our oceans.

Historically, large scale waste is a relatively recent invention. Only a century ago, humans typically maintained the products they made or purchased so they would last for as long as possible. Durability was prized. Furniture was repaired instead of replaced, cutlery and crockery was passed down from generation to generation, clothing was mended, and shoes were cobbled. But as economies sought to rebound after World War II, production shifted to disposable products following the model of planned obsolescence (extract, manufacture, use briefly, discard, repeat). Industries, economies and landfills thrived. Plastic was mass-produced at little cost, and turned into everyday goods that were previously considered luxuries. From here, the spiral fuelled itself. As economies expanded and cheaper products became available, the global population grew, bringing even more consumption, growth and waste.

Today, few manufacturers see little incentive to design anything other than disposables. However, most used products and packaging produced today can be repurposed or recycled, but other than glass, paper, certain plastics and certain metals, they are called and treated as "non-recyclable".

It ultimately comes down to a simple formula: if the cost to collect, sort and recycle a used product or package is greater than the cost of virgin materials,

'IN THE NAME OF PROFIT, INSTEAD OF DESIGNING AWAY PROBLEMS, WE HAVE MASTERED THE ART OF DOING THE INVERSE'

the used product or package is trashed, and new products are made from virgin materials. The environmental and health costs are considered external to the production equation – despite the impact of the linear economy on our life support systems (water, air, soil and carbon balance) and longer term economic impacts. Thus, trillions of candy wrappers, cigarette butts, coffee capsules and endless other disposables end up being burned in an incinerator or landfilled, where they slowly decompose over hundreds of years, releasing carbon and methane.

And here's another revelation: from an environmental perspective, incineration (converting waste to energy, which is conveniently considered a form of recycling in many corners of the "advanced" world), is not much better than landfilling. Like durable products, recycling may cost more in the short-term, but from a systems perspective it is better for the environment and economy longer term.

Yet, there is room for optimism. The more we can see the value in our waste (i.e. the more useful we can make it), the more likely it is that we can profitably collect and reprocess it. Once an object moves from being something we don't want (and that we'll pay to get rid of) to something that we want to buy, it transforms (although different laws apply) into something that is no longer considered waste.

The root cause of our current situation is in the design of our products, however a possible incentive could be to tax firms with hard-to-recycle materials like blended plastics or coated paper, while subsidising those companies using highly recoverable materials like aluminum, glass and uncoated paper.

Before that happens however, our most important step is to rethink how we buy our goods. We can start by making thoughtful, conscious purchasing decisions, and voting with our hard-earned money. We can eliminate disposable products and packaged goods that create waste, and instead opt for durable items which may cost a little more, but last longer and can be recycled. At other times the most environmentally responsible purchasing decision can be the one that never occurs – by resisting the temptation to purchase something in the first place. Among the circular solutions available to us, simply reusing something is the easiest to adopt – such as selling or acquiring a secondhand product from a thrift store, thus ensuring any usable pre-owned goods are delivered to a person or institution that will give them additional life. Meanwhile, upcycling – like turning a mason jar into a candleholder – gives waste material a value, just not the purpose it was originally designed for. We can recycle almost everything else by valuing the material an object is made from and choosing to prioritise purchasing goods made from recycled materials or in recyclable packaging.

With scale and a systemic perspective, most waste on the planet can be solved circularly and (in the long run) economically. The global movement to a Circular Economy, with luminaries from Bill McDonough to Ellen McArthur, is bringing powerful leadership and tools to companies around the world – jumpstarting the shift from the Linear Economy to a Circular Economy on a major scale.

In reflecting on the Golden Rule, let's take into account two

'IF WE TRULY EMBRACE THE GOLDEN RULE, WE'D ONLY ALLOW BACK INTO NATURE'S SYSTEM THESE ELEMENTS FROM OUR OUTPUTS THAT ARE HARMONIOUS WITH NATURE'

distinct perspectives. The first is that of our fellow humans, many of whom are greatly affected by our current waste disposal system: from drinking contaminated water (resulting from improper waste disposal), to methane emissions escaping our landfills, to the air pollution caused by our incinerators. Millions lack the economic freedom to move away from these locations and thus find themselves (and their children) face-to-face with our useless outputs on a daily basis.

Secondly, let's remember that waste doesn't exist in Nature, where remarkably every output – be it animal waste or decomposing plants, fungi and algae – becomes a useful input to a different organism. A bird may eat a seed from a plant, then a fox may eat that bird, which will one day die and be eaten by

microbes, the output from which a plant will grow, and that plant may produce a seed that another bird may eat. What outputs we bring to the world may ultimately come back to us in our food, air and water, but without doubt affect other forms of life to which we are interdependent and interconnected.

If we truly embrace the Golden Rule, we'd only allow back into Nature's system these elements from our outputs that are harmonious with Nature. Toward that lofty goal, and until we achieve it, it's all the more important to reduce, reuse and recycle.

A HUMAN
TOUCH

By Dov Seidman, Founder and Chief Executive Officer of LRN

EVERYTHING
IS PERSONAL

IN NOVEMBER OF 2014, a cyberattack against Sony Pictures released the private emails of then-co-Chair, Amy Pascal, and other company executives. Suddenly, the private thoughts and inappropriate jokes of relatively powerful people were headlines plastered across media, leading to Pascal's resignation and a black eye for the company. Remember, of course, that these people were the victims.

In July of 2015, a Milan-based cyber-security group called the Hacking Team was itself hacked, revealing a paper trail that linked their listening and surveillance technology to some of the most oppressive regimes on earth. Then, in April of 2016, the Panama Papers – stolen files documenting the creation and ownership of shell corporations from a single law firm in the central American country – were released, leading to the resignation of the Prime Minister of Iceland, badly damaging the credibility of then-UK Prime Minister, David Cameron, and revealing the financial sources of powerful, secretive regimes in Russia, China, and even North Korea.

Roughly two centuries ago, the Scottish philosopher David Hume observed that our moral imagination diminishes with distance. It follows, then, that as the world's distance is removed by spreading communications technology, the moral imagination should only increase to the point of always-on moral activation. A world without distance is like a crowded theatre, but that doesn't have to be a bad thing. Today, everything is personal. We experience the aspirations, hopes, frustrations, and plights of others in direct and visceral ways.

It is not just that the world has changed. It has been dramatically reshaped. Our world has rapidly gone from being connected, to interconnected, to interdependent. When the world is tied together this intimately, everyone's values and behaviour matter more than ever, because our actions – how we do what we do as individuals and organisations – affect more people in more ways than ever before.

'We continue to operate under the false assumption that we can create and sustain separate spheres for our personal and professional lives'

Despite this, we continue to operate under the false assumption that we can create and sustain separate spheres for our personal and professional lives. Think of the famous line from The Godfather, often used in the corporate world: "It's not personal. It's strictly business." This alone speaks volumes, but it is not that business has become immoral, or of bad morality. It has become amoral – unconcerned with and separated from morality, which is perhaps an even more unnatural and unsustainable position.

Worse still, we scaled this condition until it became so commonplace that for many of us it now feels normal. I've attended funerals where I have heard that the deceased was a "ruthless negotiator" but a "caring husband" and, people say, "not a bad guy." Business decided that it could create a separate sphere in which bosses would tell people to, "just do it, I don't care how".

However, the way the world is constructed today directly conflicts with the amoral business environment we have built. An amoral strategy is unsustainable. In an interdependent world, we have no choice but to connect with the norms, principles, and moral values that guide constructive and sustainable behaviours.

Moral values are, in fact, at the heart of capitalism. Adam Smith laid the foundations of capitalist theory, yet – contrary to what many have come to believe – he was not an economist. He was a moral philosopher. Adam Smith never used the word "capitalism," but instead talked about a system that balanced morality and natural liberties. In this sense, capitalism (as conceived by Smith) was less about the unabashed pursuit of profit than the creation of a mutual relationship between human beings.

To Smith, market success was defined by collaboration and sustainable relationships. In order to truly scale this original, moral capitalism, then, we need to build a system that provides individuals with the greatest liberty and freedom to do the right thing by following the Golden Rule: "Do unto others as you would have them do unto you."

Smith understood that companies and economies would succeed by scaling and systematising liberty – but the right kind of liberty. That means not just 'Freedom From' command and control management practices, but the 'Freedom To' innovate, to fail without fear of disproportionate consequences, to express dissent, and to be yourself regardless of your religious or cultural identity.

These factors require us to fundamentally rethink how we lead, govern, and operate our countries and organisations – designing models and solutions specifically crafted for a morally interdependent world. We must embrace and forge healthy interdependencies that are about how we treat each other. They are about behaviour that is based in values that animate and sustain human relationships, and are, in turn, the new source of competitive advantage in the Human Economy.

What do I mean by the Human Economy? Economies get labeled according to the work people predominantly do in them. The Industrial Economy replaced the Agrarian Economy when people left farms for factories; then the Knowledge Economy pulled them from factories to office buildings. When that happened, the way workers added value changed too. Instead of leveraging their brawn, companies capitalised on their brains. No longer hired hands, they were hired heads.

In the Human Economy, technology has once again caused a shift in what is most valuable. Today we hire for hearts, for the deepest, most human qualities that no machine can replicate; capacities and qualities like grit, empathy, and creativity, and values like honesty, trust, and responsibility – the elements that build relationships. That's no

coincidence. Due to our interdependence we are all in this together, whether we like it or not.

Leaders who want these deep qualities must give deeply from themselves. This requires that we stop to reassess our methods and mindsets, and innovate our approach to leadership in order to thrive.

1 The first step on this journey is to pause. It might seem counterintuitive, but in our fast-paced world nothing is more important. The act of pausing creates an oasis of composure amid the chaos, allowing us to sharpen our awareness. With refined focus, we can connect our consciousness with our conscience and truly begin to understand and embody our values. Active pausing is the heart of ethical decision-making and reliable leadership because it encourages reflection and stops us from acting based on knee-jerk reactions. In this sense, pausing is the key to truly utilising free will.

2 Second, we must embrace the notion that competitive advantage has shifted from what we do to how we do what we do. The fact that customers can instantly compare price, features, quality, and service requires leaders to fundamentally rethink how their organisations operate and how their people conduct business. Anyone can easily peer into the innermost workings of companies and governments. This means we must now ask more of our employees than we ever did in the past. We must ask them to embody their company's values in all of their behaviours in and out of the office – in tweets, blog posts, emails, or any other social interaction.

3 Third, we need to understand that the days of leading via one-way conversations are over. When Netflix raised its prices in 2011 with a one-way announcement, 800,000 customers fled. After their

CEO, Reed Hastings, apologised and admitted he'd "slid into arrogance" the company thrived – growing to over 86m subscribers as of October 2016. When a Scottish girl decided to blog about the poor quality of her school lunches in June 2012, school officials tried to shut down her site. Only after thousands of supporters amplified her cause online did a conversation result in changed policies and more nutritious offerings at her school. Leaders must be prepared to listen to their constituents, and their employees, as they now hold more power than ever.

Fourth, we must build healthy interdependencies, so we rise more and fall less together. It is our responsibility to build new coalitions – even with former competitors – as we eschew zero-sum competition and focus on the word competere, which means to strive together.

Fifth, we need to elevate and not just shift behaviour. Leaders who understand the conditions of interdependence are asking their employees to go beyond simply serving customers to exercising collaboration and creativity in all their activities at work. We ask teachers to create a sense of curiosity in the classroom and doctors to show compassion at a patient's bedside. The qualities we truly desire can only be inspired in employees who consider the company's mission and values worthy of their dedication. And that can only happen when employees have a sense that their work "means something" and provides value to the larger world.

Sixth, we need to change how we measure progress. The adage that "you manage what you measure" remains valid, but traditional measures are not sufficient in today's world. We painstakingly continue to track GDP, revenue, debt, risk, friends, votes, followers, and engagement, yet revenues are flat, debt has never been higher, risk has never loomed larger, and engagement scores are at an all-time low. In an interdependent world, we need a reliable method for measuring how we forge healthy interdependencies, how organisations operate and relate to society, the way in which they treat their people, and how their staff behave and treat others.

Seventh, we need to learn to extend trust instead of just inspecting for it. The value of trust lies in finding ways to give it away. A New York City doughnut maker boosted his productivity and profits after he trusted his customers to calculate their own change, illustrating the inspired behaviours that flow from extending trust. Trust inspires others to take the risks that are essential to spurring innovation.

Finally, leaders must recognise that as power shifts to individuals, leadership itself must shift with it: from coercive leadership that extracts performance and allegiance out of people to inspirational leadership that fosters commitment and innovation. This shift is part of an evolving global trend – one that especially resonates with the rising millennial generation, whose members are already demonstrating their moral authority. At age 15, Sarah Kavanagh convinced Pepsi and Coca-Cola to stop using carcinogenic brominated vegetable oil in their sports drinks. Julia Bluhm, at the same age, convinced Seventeen Magazine to ban photoshopped images of young girls. These young leaders didn't buy large shares of stock or threaten boycotts. They simply assembled petitions and made it clear to those companies where their customers' values stood. Their actions were inspired by a deep commitment to improving the world.

This is the direction in which the whole world is moving, and it leaves leaders with a distinct choice: adapt and thrive or fade away.

If you incorporate the seven principles I've listed above into your behaviour, you will have played your part in spreading the most powerful innovation for our new reality: The Human Operating System.

'Purpose lies at the heart of the Human Operating System'

When Microsoft Word was competing for dominance with Word Perfect, Bill Gates' built the Windows Operating System so that apps like Word, Excel, PowerPoint, and Outlook could work together to increase productivity. By analogy, in the Human Economy the apps we need are elevated human behaviours. Thus, we need a Human Operating System that allows us to better access them.

Purpose lies at the heart of the Human Operating System. In this system, governance that maximises short-term, commercial interests and only measures "how much" business gets done is replaced with governance that embraces responsibility to society, long-term goals, and also measures how business gets done. It is a system with a culture of shared values and principles that guide what people should and should not do. When taken to full scale across industries, this would create the opposite effect of The Godfather – from the amoral business world many of us grew up in, to restoring capitalism to a system of liberties as originally conceived by Adam Smith.

Whether in business or the non-profit world, the first job of leaders is to get the culture right. The real power to change and shape the behaviour of others comes from setting a collective ethos of shared expectation. Building the Human Operating System allows organisations to do great things because it is the kind of system that allows for both resilience and growth. It is flexible because it runs on empathy. It is propulsive because it runs on sustainable human energy and shared trust.

The more leaders become deliberate about the example they set through all their actions and the approach they take to connecting and collaborating with their colleagues, the more a general atmosphere of compassion will be built. This human touch necessarily returns morality to business and, with that, helps us create a deep connection to our most sincere beliefs and values. When we do this, we can contribute to building a better world.

FINANCIALLY
LATE

REFORM OF THE BANKING SYSTEM WILL TAKE ANOTHER 10 YEARS

**By Antony Jenkins,
Former CEO Barclays**

READERS OF THIS JOURNAL might permit themselves a wry smile when encountering an essay on banking. Wasn't this the industry that, driven by greed, brought about the biggest economic recession in human history? That forced the world to the edge of the abyss of a global depression from which there could be no recovery? That caused millions to lose their jobs and homes? And through the draconian actions required of policy-makers, accelerated the growth in inequality; those with few or no assets experienced a reduction in real income, while those with assets benefited from a considerable increase in the value of those assets driven by quantitative easing. In fact, wasn't this the industry that was too aggressive, too self-serving and too short-termist and therefore the very opposite of compassionate?

As someone who has worked in financial services for over 30 years, in many different parts of the world, I have observed all the above. Even the language used by some in the industry is anathema to compassion: "a zero sum game", "the greater fool theory", or "you eat what you kill".

Eight years on from the financial crisis, many will say little has changed. Customers are at best ambivalent towards banks (as measured by customer satisfaction) and levels of complaints remain stubbornly high. Shareholders are still not receiving a return on equity above the cost of equity in most European banks. Constant rounds of job reduction can hardly make banks an inspiring place to work and trust in the sector has never been lower as scandal after scandal has emerged and fines have skyrocketed.

True, changes in regulation have made improvements to the capital, leverage and liquidity positions of banks and this process will continue into the next decade, but these alone will not create a system that society deserves; one that meets customers' needs, is cost-effective, fair, transparent and secure, and finally, one that delivers reasonable returns to shareholders.

This really matters to individuals and to society. For the individual, I always remind staff that there is nothing inherently valuable in banking services and that they are often a chore for the customer. But what these services enable in those customers' lives is profound. Getting a mortgage is time-consuming but buying a home is often life-changing. Applying for a business loan may involve a lot of paperwork but taking that enterprise to the next level by launching a new product, entering a new market or employing more people, is profound.

For society, an effective and fair banking system is a necessary condition for sustained and viable economic growth, and without economic growth, it is difficult for citizens to enjoy a higher quality of life. More economic growth means more and varied employment opportunities, more tax revenues to fund education and healthcare, and greater levels of home ownership.

We have a banking system that is flawed and remains so after the crisis. The solution must be to create a system that acts compassionately to serve individuals and society. Where the individuals who work within it, regulate it and profit from it through the provision of capital, treat others as they would wish to be treated themselves.

In wrestling with this question over many years, I can assure you there are no easy answers. This is not about the elimination of the profit motive, for surely banks have performed very poorly for their shareholders post-2008. No doubt better-run banks would not have incurred so many charges for past misconduct, and would have addressed the fundamental shift in business model required to deliver decent returns to those shareholders, if the profit motive were more operative in these institutions.

Nor is this about size and complexity inherently, although I do accept that this does not always help. Banks of all shapes and sizes failed during the crisis, the reason for which was predominantly poorly understood and priced risk which ultimately crystallised into losses which could not be absorbed by low capital levels.

But I would suggest that there are five core principles, that if applied consistently and with discipline, will produce a more compassionate banking system: one that society deserves.

1

Firstly, banks must serve all stakeholders in the short and the long-term. Like all businesses, banks exist to serve their customers, provide rewarding work for their employees, deliver on their responsibilities to society and thus generate acceptable returns to providers of capital, usually shareholders. These interests are potentially in conflict and must be continuously harmonised in the short and long-term. Where leaders focus excessively on one dimension such as driving short-term profits through aggressive sales techniques, for example in Payment Protection Insurance or over rewarding employees through unjustifiably high levels of compensation, customers and shareholders pay the price over the long-term. The reverse is also true of course and the harmonisation of these interests over the short and long-term is the key to a successful and sustainable organisation.

2

Secondly, define your goal, purpose and values. People come to work for a variety of reasons: to support their family, to grow as a professional, to make a difference, to be part of something bigger than themselves. Very few people, but admittedly some in financial services, define the value of their work in purely financial terms which is, of course, morally bankrupt but also soul-destroying.

For those people, there will always be someone paid more than them and therefore they are doomed to live in a state of constant dissatisfaction. And there are still unreconstructed aspects of our industry that are prone to doing business at all costs regardless of its appropriateness, and people who measure their status by how much they are paid.

In the 50s and 60s bank managers seemed steadfast and rather dull, while merchant bankers were more entrepreneurial and risk-taking, but operated as partnerships. That worked because society had an effective commercial banking system and a merchant banking system where risk-taking was moderated by the fact that it was the partner's own money at stake.

'WE HAVE A BANKING SYSTEM THAT IS FLAWED. THE SOLUTION MUST BE TO CREATE A SYSTEM THAT ACTS COMPASSIONATELY'

Post the deregulation of the 80s, commercial banks operated increasingly as retailers focusing on volume while merchant banks became companies where the shareholders' money was at risk. These changes led to a fundamental failure to focus on the customer on the one hand and the shareholder on the other.

Then, as merchant banks became investment banks, that led to a 'pile 'em high, sell 'em cheap' mentality and, although it may have worked for retailers, it did not work for banks.

But, as we know, human beings don't like change and anything that has taken 30 years to be created won't be rolled back in just five years or even ten. Instead some of the limits may come from outside influences, where we have witnessed regulatory change, amongst wider changes in technology and the whole economic environment that may have a more profound effect.

I think when the industry worked in partnerships there was general acknowledgement that it was a more sustainable system. Setting a clear goal for the organisation and defining an existential purpose supported by well-defined values is also a way of orienting the organisation around compassion.

Through the use of a balanced scorecard setting goals for stakeholders over time, this can also be made tangible for colleagues in terms of what must be done and how it should be done. Behaviour can then be encouraged through performance management systems, promotion mechanisms and compensation structures. At Barclays, we set our goal as becoming the 'Go-to bank', our purpose as 'helping people achieve their ambitions in the right way' and our values as 'respect, integrity, service, excellence and stewardship'. All of this was backed up by a set of eight five-year goals, two for each of our stakeholders.

3

Thirdly, build the right leadership and culture. Now, the above is all very well but it really is about what you do, not what you say. Barclays famously installed the values on massive transparent signage in the lobby of the headquarters building, but this was only a communications exercise to drive awareness amongst colleagues. Leadership and its transmission to the organisation through culture is the only way to ensure compassionate outcomes. The behaviours of leaders must be consistent with the goal, purpose and values. The organisation will see in an instant any lack of authenticity and consistency, while culture must be constantly managed and nurtured by the actions of all employees.

This is hard, demanding work, and requires time. I believe that such a journey takes a minimum of five years and probably closer to ten. This, of course, requires consistency of support from the board and a high level of execution from management.

It is also important that leadership address the 'bad actor' problem. In any large organisation there will likely be those who act with bad intent, for example, in fraudulently moving money from a customer's account to one they control or in manipulating reference rates such as LIBOR. Culture alone will not protect against such behaviour, although it will clearly create a less conducive environment for it. A strong culture must be supplemented with effective protective and detective controls that root out and appropriately punish the bad actor, established and enforced by leadership.

4

Fourthly, have courage. One of the most significant learnings for me in recent years has been the role of the individual in creating the profound change required to build compassionate banking. As individuals, we are programmed to be suspicious of, and to resist, change. It is an emotional reaction much more powerful than any logic that justifies the need for change. One of the reasons why organisations generally respond more effectively in a crisis is because the urgency of the crisis overcomes the fear that would usually create inaction. I truly believe that I would not have been able to introduce goals, purpose and values at Barclays had it not been for the massive collapse in the reputation of the organisation following the LIBOR scandal.

Now clearly it is unrealistic to create a permanent sense of crisis in order to drive profound change, but I believe much more time needs to be spent working with individual leaders to help them understand their own fears and how to overcome them so that they can lead change more effectively. In many ways this is about acting compassionately within organisations in order to build commitment to the change agenda and improve the effectiveness of its execution.

5

Finally, society must establish the right regulation. I have argued that it is in a bank's own interest to create a compassionate banking system, but it is also right that society should ensure that banks operate appropriately through the setting and policing of regulation. To be clear, this cannot be a substitute for a bank's responsibilities, but it must be a critical last line of defence. While much progress has been made on improving capital and liquidity levels within banks, a process of further optimisation will be required. Further, on conduct regulation, a more comprehensive description of the rights and responsibilities of the customer and the bank is appropriate so each party can clearly benefit from the relationship.

In my view, with the implementation of these five principles, it is possible to construct a banking system with compassion at its heart that serves customers, colleagues, shareholders and society in the right way.

There are some grounds for optimism in the aspiration I see amongst some industry leaders to accomplish this, but there are also leaders who believe that the impetus for change will pass with a recovering global economy. *Only time will tell whether there are enough such leaders across the industry and whether they will be given the time to create a system that "banks as you would like to be banked".*

'SETTING A CLEAR GOAL FOR THE ORGANISATION AND DEFINING AN EXISTENTIAL PURPOSE SUPPORTED BY WELL-DEFINED VALUES IS ALSO A WAY OF ORIENTING THE ORGANISATION AROUND COMPASSION'

FAIR TRADING

By Steve Waygood, Chief Responsible Investment Officer, Aviva Investors

FAIRTRADE FOR FINANCE. In finance, in order for us to do unto others as we would like others to do unto us, we must first know what our money is actually doing unto others.

Let's imagine for a moment a financial system that is well-understood. What does this look like? We are aware of what corporate activity we are funding. We know whether we agree with what these companies are doing and how they are behaving.

We are aware of how our influence over the companies we own has been promoting sustainable business and we understand how our insurance, savings and investment products work. In this compassionate capitalist system we know how to hold our fund managers to account and what they are doing with our money.

The capital markets are arguably the most important global markets, shaping the daily reality of billions of people and the wellbeing of future generations. However, very few of the non-professionals have anything even approaching a modest understanding of how it works.

This is largely because the system is hardly ever taught. It is not in national curricula. It is rarely included in undergraduate or even post-graduate qualifications. Indeed, it is possible to do an MBA and not understand how capital originates with individuals, or know which institutions it flows through before being put to work in the real economy.

This surprising state of affairs continues because it is not in the short-term financial interests of professional industry insiders for this to change. This has in turn led to an erosion of trust in financial services.

In the economic jargon, we have a "market failure due to an asymmetry of information". Put simply, the seller knows a great deal about the product but the buyer knows very little. This is partly why there is so much regulation protecting consumers of financial services.

But, staggeringly, very little of this regulation is orientated towards our concerns about sustainability, our personal ethics or our compassion and concern for each other. In other words, nobody is upholding the Golden Rule for us, so we must take it on ourselves.

VISION

Let's imagine what might happen if we were to design capital markets that promoted sustainability, ethics and compassion. Wouldn't it be wonderful to harness the roughly $300tn that is traded on the global capital markets to support, rather than undermine, sustainable development?

From a sustainability perspective, we should start with the UN Sustainable Development Goals (SDGs), which represent the legacy we aspire to bequeath to future generations and the planet. These can be considered alongside the Paris Agreement on Climate Change as being among the most positive geopolitical multilateral achievements of our century so far.

Delivering success is a joint responsibility for all of us and we each have our own part to play. For example, governments and inter-governmental institutions can act as catalysts for change – enabling and incentivising business and civil society to correct the market failures which stand in the way of more long-term and sustainable behaviour. But what is the role of finance here?

'Delivering success is a joint responsibility for all of us and we each have our own part to play'

THE SOCIAL USEFULNESS OF FINANCE

For the last decade, I have been lucky enough to work at Aviva, one of the world's largest insurance companies. Insurers should be good stewards and we have gone to considerable lengths to promote good corporate governance and corporate responsibility as this drives both long-term profitability and real world improvements for people and sustainable development.

We also understand how important it is for our license to operate so that our clients understand what we do and trust that we think carefully about our social contribution.

Yet currently the financial supply chain is not working to deliver the ambition enshrined in the SDGs and we believe the markets need to be brought onto a more sustainable footing, so we can mobilise private sector finance to support their delivery.

We consider that not delivering the UN SDGs would be the world's most significant market failure and consequently, we have given some thought to how this could be achieved.

SOLUTIONS

In July 2014 we published a Roadmap for Sustainable Capital Markets, which sought to help the policy-makers at the United Nations understand capital markets and begin to ensure that the $300tn was used to support the SDGs. In the context of compassionate capitalism, there are three related ideas that help awareness and understanding which I would like to build on here:

1. Free league tables benchmarking corporate performance on the SDGs. This would move us closer to our opening vision of knowing what the companies we own are doing and how they are behaving.

2. Standards for sustainable investment. This moves us towards our vision that our influence over the companies we own has been used positively.

3. Sustainable finance literacy in the national curriculum. A third step that helps us understand how to hold our fund managers to account and assures us we are aware of what they are doing with our money.

Let's look at these in more detail.

1. BENCHMARKS RANKING CORPORATE PERFORMANCE ON THE SDGS

The institutional investment industry has witnessed a quiet revolution in the area of Environmental, Social and corporate Governance (ESG) data disclosure by companies in the past decade.

However, it is not yet motivating the improvements we need to see in corporate sustainability performance, and certainly not on the scale required, which would unlock the trillions in the capital markets.

There are several reasons for this. The data is hard to digest and does not adhere to clear standards, while almost all the analysis is privately held, costs money to access, and is therefore not widely used. Yet, this type of data should be a public good. On the occasions when civil society does get access to the analysis, they tend not to trust it or to understand the analytical framework. Consequently, there is not enough pressure on companies, either from investors or from civil society, to improve their corporate sustainability performance.

The solution is to develop a set of publicly available, corporate sustainability bench-marks, or league tables, ranking companies on their performance across a range of indicators such as climate change, gender equality, labour standards, access to healthcare and other indicators aligned to the SDGs. The building of the benchmarks should be collaborative, with input provided by companies, civil society, investors and independent rating providers on the methodology. The benchmarks would harness the ESG data that companies increasingly disclose and for the first time enable companies, policymakers, civil society and retail investors to quickly and easily compare the relative performance of companies within a sector, over time, on a range of business-relevant SDGs. These benchmarks could be summarised in a dashboard ranking corporate performance across the SDG benchmarks, so enhancing comparability further.

The benchmarks would create competitive pressure and it's this and the increased transparency that would provide such a powerful incentive for companies to improve their performance. Our own experience as investors also tells us that companies that consider long-term sustainability are ultimately more successful, which benefits the companies themselves as well as the wider economy.

The UK International Development Committee recommended recently that the UK government should support the development of international benchmarks against the SDGs to enable companies to monitor and report on their progress against relevant targets. This is a hugely welcome development which will provide an important cata-lyst for changes that contribute to the long-term health of a business and make visible efforts towards sustainable development.

The UK government has taken important first steps in this regard already. In 2014, Aviva partnered with other investors, research agencies and civil society organisations to develop the Corporate Human Rights Benchmark (CHRB), which will publicly rank the top 500 globally listed companies on their human rights policy, process and perfor-mance, using the UN Guiding Principles on Business and Human Rights as a framework. By publishing results, this will harness the competitive nature of

the market to drive better human rights performance. The benchmark has received backing from the UK and Dutch governments.

This benchmark is easily replicated across sectors. It is a market-led, non-legislative solution that will help to ensure finance flows become consistent with sustainable development. Although business-led, there is also a clear role for policy-makers to provide an enabling environment.

The funding model will be central to success as the results will be given away for free. The costs of research and analysis will need to be covered, and this will be a significant challenge. We believe the benchmarks will cost in the order of $25-30m to produce, and could be built and running within three years. As the results are a public good and free at the point of use, we would hope that enlightened governments, foundations and capitalists will come together to fund the work. Experience with the CHRB to date demonstrates that this is a realistic ambition.

'In a compassionate capitalist system, we will know how to hold our fund managers to account and will be aware of what they are doing with our money'

2. SUSTAINABLE FINANCE BENCHMARKS

Voluntary standards in other industries are commonplace (such as Fairtrade in the retail sector) but there is no equivalent for the finance industry. I believe that a kite-mark should be developed to accredit standards in responsible investment – effectively a 'Fairtrade for Finance' – so that companies can differentiate themselves on responsible investment and investors can make informed, responsible investment decisions.

How could this be achieved? The International Organisation for Standardisation and its national equivalents such as the British Standards Institute could work with the World Resources Institute and the Fairtrade Foundation to lead the development of auditable voluntary standards regarding sustainable investment.

Our initial conversations with these institutions suggest that there is considerable interest in this. The International Corporate Governance Network and the UN-supported Principles for Responsible Investment should be invited to support the technical aspects of the creation of such a standard. A number of leading fund managers should also be invited alongside a range of stakeholders onto the technical working committee. The standard should be voluntary and, as asset owners include it in their due diligence reviews, it would enable them to see through the smoke and mirrors where not many fund managers claim to be responsible.

Relevant uses include in investment analysis, company engagement as owners and the integration of the benchmark into their voting decisions at company annual general meetings. For example, if the gender equality benchmark demonstrates that a company has done poorly on promoting equality, then the fund manager may wish to vote against the bonus of the director in charge. To make progress with the kite-mark, this initiative would require a degree of political and financial support. We estimate that the work would require approximately £150,000 ($220,000) and take up to two years to complete.

3. SUSTAINABLE FINANCE LITERACY

Investor stewardship is vital to the long-term success of companies and the economy as a whole. However, a lack of financial literacy amongst end-investors about how financial markets work and how they impact people's pensions and the wider world means that demand for good stewardship is low. As fund managers for example, our retail customers rarely ask how we incorporate ESG data into our investment decisions and pension trustees often lack the skills to consider such information.

The gap in understanding how finance works is a profound problem for sustainable development as it permeates short-termism throughout the financial markets and directs capital away from sustainable investments. One of the solutions to improving financial literacy would be for governments to make it a core component of the school curriculum. This should go beyond basic money management and include an understanding of how markets impact upon people's lives and shape the world around us. The Organisation for Economic Cooperation and Development's review of financial literacy in 2018 may be a good opportunity to promote greater understanding in schools.

CAVEAT EMPTOR

Some readers may be left thinking that these three ideas are not enough. I agree. The primary failure of the capital markets is a result of the failure of global governments to properly internalise environmental and social costs into companies' profit and loss statements.

As a consequence, the capital markets do not incorporate companies' full social and environmental costs. Indeed, until these market failures are corrected through government intervention of some kind, unsustainable companies will continue to have a lower cost of capital than they should and so are more likely to be financed than sustainable companies.

If the economy is to be moved onto a truly sustainable basis, then we would expect to see governments taking action to correct the many distortions in the pricing systems on fisheries, freshwater, climate change and natural resource depletion. This is how sustainability issues become relevant to our corporate valuation work, and this is how our capital is put to work in the right places. This requires, for example, setting regulatory performance standards, creating fiscal measures such as carbon taxes, or setting up market mechanisms such as carbon trading schemes that price the externalities and ensure that the negative externalities are corrected.

Some related reforms have already taken place and been proven to work successfully like the Sustainable Stock Exchanges Initiative, launched in 2008, and the Global Reporting Initiative, founded in 1997. However, for compassionate capitalism to work, financial services clients wanting to adopt the Golden Rule in finance need to continue to show both an increased awareness and understanding.

CONCLUSION

In a compassionate capitalist system, we will know how to hold our fund managers to account and will be aware of what they are doing with our money. These are three suggestions towards a vision of compassionate capitalism.

First, benchmarks will help us know whether we agree with what corporate activity we are funding and how they are behaving. Second, sustainable finance standards will inform our awareness of how our influence over the companies we own has been promoting sustainable business. And third, sustainable finance education and its inclusion in the national curriculum will help current and future generations understand how insurance, savings and investment products work.

The combination of all three will enable us to know what our money is doing unto others and we can all then ensure it is doing what we would like others to do unto us.

A BRIEF HISTORY OF THE GOLDEN RULE

1800 BC

EGYPT

"Eloquent Peasant" story contains the first closest version
Do to the doer to cause that he do

563-483 BC

BUDDHA

(Dhammapada, Northern Canon, 5:18)
Hurt not others with what pains yourself

551-479 BC

CONFUCIUS

(Analects 15:23)
Don't do to others what you don't want them to do to you

500 BC

TAOISM IN CHINA

Regard your neighbour's gain as your gain and your neighbour's loss as your loss

400 BC

HINDU

(Mahabharata bk. 13: Anusasana Parva, 113)
In happiness and misery, in the agreeable and the disagreeable, one should judge effects as if they came to one's own self

30 BC - 10 AD

JUDAISM

(Rabbi Hillel in Sanhedrin of the Babylonian Talmud 56a)

What is hateful to yourself, don't do to another. That is the whole Torah. The rest is commentary

4 BC - 65 AD

CHRISTIANITY

Christianity (Bible, Matthew 7:12)

Treat others as you want to be treated, for this sums up the Law and the prophets

222-235

ROMAN EMPEROR ALEXANDER SEVERUS

Adopts the Golden Rule, displaying it on public buildings

610

MUHAMMAD

(Via several Hadiths: Bukhari 1:2:12, Muslim 1:72f, and An-Nawawi 13)

None of you is a true believer unless he wishes for his brother what he wishes for himself

1200

INCA LEADER MANCO CAPAC IN PERU

(Wattles 1996: 192)

Each one should do unto others as he would have others do unto him

1651

THOMAS HOBBES

(Leviathan, Ch. 15)

When you doubt the rightness of your action toward another, suppose yourself in the other's place

1763

VOLTAIRE

(du Roy 2008:94)

The single fundamental and immutable law for men is the following: 'Treat others as you would be treated'

1871

CHARLES DARWIN

("Descent Man")

Argues human morality evolves from a limited tribal concern to a higher, universal concern that's summed up in the Golden Rule

1897-1904

SAMUEL JONES

Mayor of Toledo, Ohio, USA runs the city on Golden Rule terms

1900

PROVERB

Yoruba people, Nigeria

One who is going to take a pointed stick to pinch a baby bird should first try it on himself to feel how it hurts

1948

UNITED NATIONS

"United Nations Declaration of Human Rights"
All human beings are born free and equal in dignity and rights... and should act towards one another in a spirit of brotherhood

1948

LOS ANGELES HIGH SCHOOL

A high-school teacher conducts an experiment getting students to live the Golden Rule without telling their parents. Many later vow to live this way forever

1963

ALDOUS HUXLEY

Writer and philosopher, writes:
"It has become clear that the Golden Rule applies not only to the dealings of human individuals and societies with one another, but also to their dealings with other living creatures and the planet"

2009

"A COMMON WORD"

A book by 300 Muslim leaders and 460 organisations stresses the Islamic Golden Rule:
None of you has faith until you love for your neighbour what you love for yourself

2015

PAPAL ENCYCLICAL BY POPE FRANCIS

The Pope's second encyclical, *Laudato si'* on climate change, states:
The Golden Rule points us in a clear direction. Let us treat others with the same passion and compassion with which we want to be treated. Let us seek for others the same possibilities which we seek for ourselves. Let us help others to grow, as we would like to be helped ourselves

ONE DOLLAR

By Dr. Mohammed 'Mo' Ibrahim, Founder and Chairman of the Mo Ibrahim Foundation

TIME FOR TRANSPARENCY. Eleven years ago, in May 2005, we concluded the sale of 'Celtel', a mobile company I founded in 1998, to build and operate mobile networks across Sub-Saharan Africa, an idea many of my colleagues thought was ill-thought, if not crazy. Telecom operators shunned the African market as a risky environment.

In various discussions I had with my colleagues in the industry about the aversion to investment in Africa, the common thread was concern about corruption, rule of law and unpredictability (read here military coups, unrest, instability, etc.)

It was sobering to watch first-hand how the reputation of a continent (whether deserved or exaggerated) can hold back investment in crucial infrastructure and damage the prospects of a whole continent.

I always believed that the story of corruption in Africa is incomplete. It is usually told by Western businessmen and naturally it

misses the part played by those very business people in fostering the practice. In Africa we have a proverb which says the true story of the hunt can only be told when the lions learn to write.

In one of our early board meetings of Celtel, we had extensive discussions of bribery and how, as a company, we should deal with it. It was easy to state 'not a single dollar' policy, but how to implement and enforce the policy? It was essential to support the field managers of our operations. These are the people who could come under pressure in some countries, not our board members. I proposed we limit the financial powers of our executives to only $30,000 of any expenditure outside the board approved budget.

The instruction went to our CEOs, if you come under pressure from the 'power', you can truthfully say you need board approval. That simple solution proved effective in the very few cases when some political leader demanded support (a nicer word than bribery).

Once it became known that Celtel did not provide 'support', we were never bothered again. We paid our taxes in full and on time in the countries where we operated, and soon we became the largest tax payer in a few of our countries and we discovered that you don't have to pay a bribe to do business in Africa!

This experience has led me to believe that bribery in many cases is optional. If business was firm and committed to its moral principles, the

89

problem will go away, but unfortunately, that is not always the case. If the true story of corruption in Africa is ever written, we will discover that, for every corrupt government official, perhaps a dozen businessmen should be beside him in the dock.

Corruption, or the perception of corruption, can deny the country, or even the continent, investment badly needed to develop, creating jobs, services and prosperity. That was a lesson I learned first-hand.

Corrupt financial practices are not limited to bribery. Actually, trade mis-invoicing is the primary means of shifting funds out of developing countries illicitly, according to a recent comprehensive study by Global Financial Integrity.

The study estimates that Sub-Saharan Africa lost over $74bn in 2013. That is more than double the amount of humanitarian and development aid it received! Illicit financial flows are not limited to Africa but are a global problem with Asia (and even developing Europe), heading the list of victims. The sums of these illicit flows are a staggering trillion dollars per year. Imagine what a trillion dollars per year can deliver in services, infrastructure, health and education for the citizens of these countries?

One of the most insidious problems is the issue of profit shifting practised by many multinational corporations which indulge in the practice of choosing where to pay their taxes. Frankly, I've been astounded at how this problem continues to grow. It hits Africa hard because of our smaller economies.

What they are doing is perfectly legal (at least for now) but it highlights one of the challenges of globalisation. Businesses, as usual, are far ahead of regulators and governments. Governments still struggle with the new global age instead of taking a collaborative approach. We watch a race to the bottom with governments competing by offering sweetheart deals to lure corporations. It is a lose-lose game.

We need solutions and the G20 needs to perfect proposals to deal with it, because I don't see action being taken yet, other than the European Commission's €13bn bill against Apple in Ireland.

Corruption and widespread financial malpractice is eroding the public trust in governments, business and institutions at a time when we need that trust.

We barely emerged from a major financial crisis, only to lurch into an uncertain economic environment with the slowdown of China, the collapse in commodities and oil prices and the rise of demagogues in the political space. These are dangerous times!

In simple terms, the Golden Rule can be our guide. We must have the courage to ensure trust between nations and between companies, meaning we treat others as we wish

'CORRUPTION, OR THE PERCEPTION OF CORRUPTION, CAN DENY THE COUNTRY OF INVESTMENT BADLY NEEDED TO DEVELOP'

to be treated, and that the transparency we desire to find in the systems of developing countries is also present in our own.

In Africa, safety and national security are being undermined as shown by my recent 'Ibrahim Index of African Governance' and we need to pay attention to achieve good governance.

We hang our coat on the issue of elections, but just holding elections is not a guarantee, in itself, of the integrity of the democratic process. We witness incumbents tinkering with the constitutions to stay in power beyond their term limits or stealing elections by forging voter registers, or the results, besides harassment of opposition and closing the space for civil society. Burundi, Congo and Uganda are just examples of what we have witnessed this year.

We must also focus on what good governance means – transparency and respecting the rights of the individual – that's what we need to strive for, not help from outside, while this 'strong man' culture needs to end.

We should also commend Africa's positive examples. I recently spoke to students at the London School of Economics, but none of them had heard of the former Namibian president Hifikepunye Pohamba or ex-Botswana President Festus Mogae, both of whom won my Ibrahim foundation's £5m prize for excellence in African governance. All our continent's criminals are celebrities in the West, yet our good people, and some of them are real heroes, often remain unknown.

A final battle is the interesting creature, 'the anonymous company', a trustee company where the beneficial ownership is hidden.

As such, it is a perfect vehicle to hide 'hot' money. If you are a corrupt official, or a drug dealer, or one of those dictators, or 'presidents for life'

variety, where would you keep your loot? Under the mattress? But that is for petty thieves. Besides, there is no mattress big enough to hide your considerable loot. A serious problem!

Don't worry, we, the civilised governments of the enlightened democracies have created a unique vehicle specially for you, 'the anonymous company'. You don't even have to travel to those distant obscure islands. Welcome to the US and Europe! There are more anonymous companies in the US than in Panama. Is that acceptable? In this day and age when we talk about good governance, transparency and rule of law, how could our governments continue to offer such havens?

Trustee companies are useful and legitimate, we need them, but the beneficial ownership should not be concealed. The leaked 'Panama Papers' were a leak from one firm in one country, but what about all firms in all countries?

That is an earthquake soon to hit us. What is needed is transparency. That includes a public register of who owns what and it requires countries worldwide to show courage and say: 'Let's do away with this!'

A lack of transparency and international cooperation and commitment are at the heart of much of the chaos we see around us today.

Our politicians have been reluctant to act. Collectively, we need them to have the guts, the moral backbone and the courage to stand up together and take these decisions.

'LACK OF INTERNATIONAL COOPERATION AND COMMITMENT IS AT THE HEART OF MUCH OF THE CHAOS WE SEE AROUND US TODAY'

DIVIDED
NATIONS

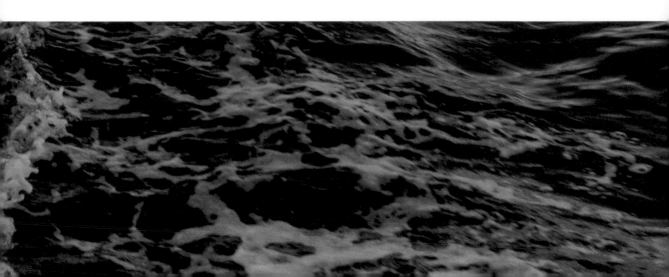

By Lord Mark Malloch-Brown, Chair of the Business
and Sustainable Development Commission

Is the UN in decline?
Is the refugee crisis
an example?

The Golden Rule of compassion is ultimately about equality, about
putting aside immediate self-interest in the recognition of a larger,
long-term common good. It is this attribute that must become the
renewed driving force of global governance if it is to survive and
succeed in the 21st century.

Compassion has always been a driving factor of international cooperation.
Many of the international institutions that exist today were founded out of
a wish to avoid further human suffering. The League of Nations, created
in the aftermath of World War I, included a Committee for Refugees,
dedicated to helping those displaced en masse by the unprecedented
conflict. Its actions included the creation of the temporary Nansen
Passport, issued to almost half a million stateless refugees during the
interwar period, in order to ensure their legal rights within states.

The end of World War II saw the creation of the United Nations,
while the 1951 Convention relating to the Status of Refugees sought to
secure legal rights for refugees in the years to come. But now it seems
that the UN, both in its refugee work and more widely, has reached an
impasse. A new Secretary-General can either revive it or preside over a
continuing, and perhaps fatal, decline.

Cold War competition, followed now by a tumultuous period of
uncertainty, has left many of these institutions reeling, along with the
states and governments they are meant to help, and whose behaviours
they are meant to curb or regulate. If we are to restore this motivating
role of compassion to international affairs today we need a robust,
respected and consistent international framework.

The European response to the growing refugee crisis is a case in
point. Asylum-seekers in Calais, many attempting to reach the U.K., have
attracted the attention of the British media, but far more refugees cross
over into other European nations on a regular basis.

IMAGINAL CELLS: VISIONS OF TRANSFORMATION | DIVIDED NATIONS

95

Closer to the epicentre of the war in Syria, the burden is many times larger. Countries like Turkey, Jordan and Lebanon have taken in a vast number of refugees. Compared to the hospitality these countries have provided, Europe's task should be a relatively easy one.

A useful figure is that only 6% of the world's refugee caseload is being hosted by Europe so, at this point, others are accepting the disproportionate burden.

Yet the response to the crisis has been divided and, in many cases, all too self-interested. While there have been many calls for compassion towards the new arrivals, especially in response to heart-rending images from the Mediterranean, this has not been matched by the only thing that could make a long-lasting difference: a consistent and widely agreed upon Europe-wide response.

It does not have to be this way. If all EU countries agreed to the same asylum standards and accepted a proportionately similar number of newcomers, on the compassionate principle that they would expect the same rights to be granted by other countries to their populations in a time of need, then asylum systems would not break down and resentments would not fester across the EU, poisoning a powerful political and humanitarian union. Europe also does not share the burden globally or even within Europe itself.

There is a need for a principled compassionate response which accepts first that both refugees and migrants have rights, but they are different rights.

'FOR THE UK, BREXIT WAS A STRANGELY PERVERSE RESULT'

Second, given the changing demographic profile of the world, with ageing populations in Europe, for example, and a very youthful Africa and Middle East, some level of migration is going to be not just morally just but economically necessary.

Five countries produce 50% of the world's refugees and 10 countries have 80% of the world's refugees, so we need real attention to the breakdown of economic services in those countries to try and build securer, more just societies that people won't be so keen to flee.

All these things are part of the solution, but what is missing is also a sort of compassionate statesmanship, which would lead to equitable solutions.

A very general framework about immigrant arrivals has been adopted at the UN, but the real risk is that it will weaken standards and lower the difference between refugees and migrants and treat both groups badly, and be utterly illiberal.

Recently we have also seen Sweden and Germany make u-turns because they can't sustain their own levels of immigration. It is a problem for Mrs. Merkel at home and a problem for Europe as a whole, while the Swedes are becoming much more restrictive.

For the UK, Brexit was also a strangely perverse result. But it was not about Eritreans, or Afghans and Syrians. It was about Polish plumbers. It is a particular madness of Britain that a country that is completely internationalised, not only in its working classes, but professional classes, hospitals, etc., somehow seized on the idea that these refugees are a burden or a cost. Immigrants are core to Britain's economic competitiveness: populating every sector of the economy.

But while individual rights are universal, it must be perfectly reasonable to have a burden-sharing system that helps stem the refugee crisis where some countries contribute money and others contribute places, depending on their location and their demographic circumstances.

Richer governments should not only fund desperately needed social services in poor countries, but also establish the kinds of long-term policies that prevent those desperate needs arising in the first place.

Part of this will be about providing a stable and well-managed environment in which business can operate ethically to help in these provisions, as it's clear that aid money can no longer solve the problems of the world, and that a more collaborative approach is needed to address the problems that are building up.

A new system is needed where Western donors could pay large amounts to Turkey or Jordan to house refugees, but similarly, and this is very much a subject of current discussion, where countries that host the refugees can think of them as possibly long-term stayers.

A major part of the system being assistance and not permanent welfare support: assistance to integrate, assimilate and become economically productive. Donors would not have to pay every year forever for Syrian refugees in Turkey, but should instead expect to pay generously over an investment period. That is a key idea.

The same applies to the world at large, and the many problems it will face in the future.

Three principles, in addition to compassion, could drive renewal of the international system. Firstly, fairness: problems and or solutions must be framed in a way where burdens are shared not shirked. Secondly, respect for agreements and precedent: solutions should, as much as possible, be consistent across similar issues. The greatest complaint in many parts of the world about the UN is an appearance of double standards. And thirdly, a renewal of its governance to make it more representative of the modern distribution of power but also inclusive of non-state voices from civil society, business and others.

Reform of the governance structures of the UN would have to start with reform of the Security Council. The great power held by the Council today is in many ways a relic of the past. But times have changed: today it is no longer tenable for the U.K., U.S., China, France and Russia to have permanent membership and veto powers on the present exclusive terms.

Reformed veto and membership rights are no magic pill for the United Nations, and more effective political structures beyond just the Security Council need to be put in place. This would mean a further renegotiation of power between the General Assembly and the Security Council, especially surrounding crucially important issues such as the selection of the Secretary General. A more balanced system, for example, might allow the Security Council to nominate prospective candidates but give the General Assembly the final right to vote and choose. A partial reform in 2016 has at least allowed candidates to appeal in General Assembly hearings. And it is probably no coincidence that the candidate, Antonio Guterres, who was viewed as having performed best, has indeed triumphed.

Many of the world's conflicts have not been aggressively mediated or resolved, and have left a vacuum that needs to be dealt with urgently. It is the Secretary General, Antonio Guterres', highest priority.

There is also the issue of a vacuum of worsening relations between the U.S. and Russia and tension between China and the U.S., which has left a very difficult environment in which to get agreement on issues,

'THE WORLD MOVES ON AND INSTITUTIONS WON'T BE HELD HOSTAGE TO OLD POWER STRUCTURES'

leaving a poisonous state of relations amongst the world's most powerful states. The world moves on and institutions won't be held hostage to old power structures.

Instead nowadays, the work and energy needed to get things done is often not carried out by the UN, but by spin-off groups who are active and use the UN as a conversing platform, with energy and leadership coming from outside. The power of the General Assembly could be elevated and empowered if it was given a tighter, sharper agenda to discuss the state of the world.

But the most important change to the UN would be to meaningfully accommodate all of the voices that come from beyond the traditional state structures of the Security Council and the General Assembly.

Modern international relations are no longer understood to be a two-dimensional affair of state governments engaging in formal relations with each other. When different countries interact now, it is through a complex web of civil society, business and non-state actors as well as governments.

The UN must operate on these different levels if it is to remain relevant, otherwise, as we are seeing now, world affairs will increasingly pass it by. All these reforms are about making the UN a place where the many voices of the world can meet, speak and listen.

The Golden Rule of compassion is ultimately about equality, about putting aside immediate self-interest in the recognition of a larger, long-term common good. This must be the renewed driving force of global governance if it is to survive and succeed in the 21st century.

IF WE WANT TO GO FAR

Globalisation has been the most powerful force in human
history for raising living standards around the world, but
it is also considered to have "unleashed dangerous
and potentially destabilising forces"

**By Paul Polman, CEO, Unilever. Chairman, World
Business Council of the Sustainable Development**

PARTNERSHIPS

In recent months we've had the Brexit vote in Britain and the Trump phenomenon in the US, with large segments of both populations revealing that they feel excluded and disillusioned.

Both events have been coupled with a concern about the direction of our modern world today; a worry many share about an economic system that isn't quite functioning for us anymore, that caters for the few and not the many.

As the world struggles to deal with up to 8,000 new refugees a day, geopolitical strife and the twin threats of runaway climate change and growing inequality, we face a growing disconnect between today's increasingly globalised world and the fragmented structure of nation-states. This is giving rise to protectionism, xenophobia, isolationism and nationalism.

Yet in struggling to react, we have also discovered that our political systems are geared more towards dealing with the symptoms than the underlying causes that affect the future of humanity.

Addressing these challenges and breaking the vicious cycle that links them therefore represents our biggest and most urgent set of priorities.

The world seems condemned to face even greater instability unless we can find effective ways to manage these new systemic risks.

It is in that context that I believe the world gave us a remarkable solution when 193 governments signed the 17 UN Sustainable Development Goals (SDGs) in New York in September 2015, just three months before the Paris Climate Agreement was made, now ratified across the world.

I was very fortunate to help participate in the formation of these goals through the work of the High Level Panel. They have a simple aim – zero poverty, but eradicating poverty in a more sustainable and equitable way.

How did all the world's nations come together to commit to such joint and meaningful action in this world of fractured politics? Clearly the urgency of the issues weighed heavily with many. Some will have been guided by self-interest. But there is no doubt that the concept of partnership in the delivery of these agreements also played a powerful role, one of the reasons why partnerships are written into the very agreement itself as Goal 17.

For while the Goals give us a framework, it is a change that can't be made without partnerships between governments, the private sector and civil society.

This willingness to work together in pursuit of a common good is an intrinsic element of the Golden Rule that has united societies for generations – and it is needed now more than ever.

It is the core that a successful sustainable development agenda is founded upon because if the other Goals identify "what" needs to be done (everything from climate action to gender equality to peace and justice) then Goal 17 answers the question of "how". Simple arithmetic also shows that it will be impossible to get there unless the private sector gets actively involved.

Implementing the Goals is estimated to have a total cost of between $3-4tn annually, and yet the money on offer from governments is only their combined yearly overseas aid budget of $140bn. This is merely 7% of the total, much of which already goes to handling the refugee crisis and very little on trying to make long-term structural reforms.

We could see this deficit rectified with the right structural reforms in place, alongside the right technology solutions and financing. Under this new plan the pay-offs will be tremendous.

In fact, there is a lot of data out there that suggests we are sitting on one of the biggest return propositions in the history of mankind.

One dollar invested in nutrition, for example, has a $6 payoff for society. One dollar invested in preventing stunting has a $17 payoff. It has been estimated that if we give women the same rights as men in the workplace then our economy could benefit to the tune of $28tn.

So this is an opportunity agenda, not a crisis of scarcity. For the first time, it gives us a road map that talks about people and about the planet. A universal plan that touches everybody.

Fortunately, a growing number of businesses recognise the need for their companies to play a bigger role. As the cost of inaction steadily begins to exceed the cost of action, more and more are committing themselves to address wider societal and environmental challenges.

But taking action requires new thinking and completely different approaches.

At Unilever, for example, our Unilever Sustainable Living Plan (USLP) has resonated widely not just because it represents a new business model, but even more so because it is underpinned by a new business philosophy. It is predicated on the notion that business can only thrive in stable and prosperous societies and that our own self-interest is best served by serving the needs of others. In essence, it is a purpose-driven approach to doing business.

'THIS WILLINGNESS TO WORK TOGETHER IN PURSUIT OF A COMMON GOOD IS AN INTRINSIC ELEMENT OF THE GOLDEN RULE THAT HAS UNITED SOCIETIES FOR GENERATIONS'

The USLP has played a vital role in the recent progress of the company – driving innovation, mitigating risks, reducing costs, energising employees and attracting talent. Yet, from the outset, we had the humility to recognise that we didn't have all the answers and (just as importantly given the size of the challenges we face) that we couldn't achieve our aims alone.

Working in partnerships has therefore been the essential thread running through everything we have done since launching the USLP. It is key, to the commitments of our individual brands for example, to drive change through social missions which leverage their unique insights and expertise. Lifebuoy, for instance, has a mission to prevent the needless deaths of children under five from diarrhoea and other diseases through the simple act of hand washing with soap. By partnering with bodies ranging from government agencies to research establishments to international NGOs, the brand is well on the way to meeting its ambition to reach a billion people with this health and hygiene message.

It also extends to the corporate level and our commitment to drive much-needed transformational change across our industry sector, because there will always be issues that are bigger than your own company. For Unilever, it includes getting out of deforestation, which accounts for a large part of global warming. By partnering initially with other global manufacturers and retailers as part of the Global Consumer Goods Forum, which helped to bring the relevant governments on board, we are together building the necessary mechanisms (such as the Tropical Forest Alliance) and public-private commitments (for example the NY Declaration on Forests) that are destined to drive change and help to eliminate illegal deforestation from global supply chains.

On an even broader scale, we see the power of partnerships in programmes like Grow Africa, formed in 2011 as part of the World Economic Forum's 'New Vision for Agriculture' initiative. This private-public partnership includes over 200 companies and 12 African governments, which have made commitments exceeding $10bn to transform agriculture and achieve food security on the continent. Already, more than 8.6m smallholder farmers have benefitted and 58,000 jobs created. Companies as diverse as DuPont, Barry Callebaut, Rabobank and Unilever have come together with African governments in an initiative that Salum Shamte of the Southern Agricultural Growth Corridor of Tanzania has heralded as "...a pioneer in catalysing, supporting and promoting different models of multi-stakeholder partnership tailored to the national agricultural agenda and market context".

These are just some of the many examples of the role partnerships play at every stage in the value chain and at every level of human activity. They are illustrative of the 'forging of new partnerships' identified as central to the delivery of the SDGs (better health and hygiene are key, for example, to the delivery of Goal 6; action against deforestation is core to Goal 13 – 'climate action').

The evidence of the impact that such partnerships can have is growing. Limited governance capacity – both nationally and globally – makes them increasingly vital. Indeed, as the SDGs recognise, we can't address our biggest challenges without them. It's about working together to be part of the transformation; where you are very transparent and you share the issues that you have, but you are also actively part of the solutions.

It's not for companies and governments to lecture each other and say: 'You should do this or you should do that'. The challenges which we face now are of a significantly larger magnitude.

Of course, we must also demand a different type of leadership, with skills for tomorrow's world, not yesterday's. Interestingly, politicians have been saying for years: 'I can't create jobs and I can't create growth.' Instead, they have created more money by introducing quantitative easing, but the return has been low. (Most of it ended up not in the real economy but in the FuFu Economy, as I call it!)

The world has been preoccupied by chasing numbers, in particular the quarterly numbers the financial community was forcing on us. But companies are not equipped to deal with these pressures. The average lifespan of a company in the US is now 17 years and it's going down, while the average tenure of a CEO has dropped to four and a half years.

Every day another company is flushed out for trying to be less bad. Whatever newspaper you take, you will read cases of investment houses manipulating accounts, or of banks manipulating Libor, or the manipulation of emission standards – all because the CEOs are trying to meet the quarterly profits for their shareholders. Instead, businesses need to think about their business models as positive contributions.

Certainly, if you are going to pursue this bigger agenda, it is true that it involves a lot of work and that you have to spend a lot of time on it - on top of running your business, which in

today's world is not easy. But we also need to change the university system, which has been very MBA-focused with a limited, silo-like mentality focused around profit and loss. We need to incorporate bigger themes around awareness, engagement, humanity and humility.

As I like to say, we are short of leaders and we are short of trees. We need to nurture them both. At the moment we are too focused on the monetary gains our leaders can bring, so perhaps we need to bring that balance back a little for the interests of the common good.

We must move instead to a mindset of partnering for the common good, founded on joint accountability and responsibility to put our businesses to the service of society, not the other way round.

Those business leaders who understand this and who, above all, have a deep appreciation of what it means to be human are addressing perhaps the most important need that humans have of other humans. This is to feel the respect of others and have their dignity protected. Those leaders are living out the Golden Rule.

As the old African proverb reminds us, "if we want to go fast go alone, but if we want to go far, go together". And we still have far to go.

'THOSE BUSINESS LEADERS WHO HAVE A DEEP APPRECIATION OF WHAT IT MEANS TO BE HUMAN ARE ADDRESSING PERHAPS THE MOST IMPORTANT NEED HUMANS HAVE OF OTHER HUMANS. THOSE LEADERS ARE LIVING OUT THE GOLDEN RULE'

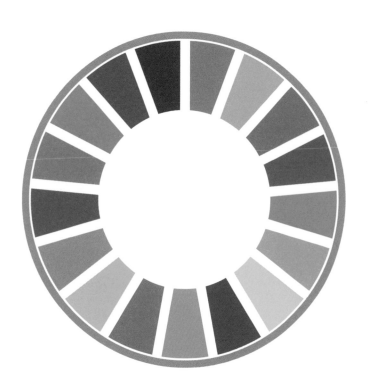

THE GLOBAL GOALS
For Sustainable Development

WE'VE

"If you would like to have opportunities for yourself, create opportunities for others."

JOBS

Oxfam has been releasing increasingly concerning updates on wealth concentration each year. In 2016, the charity told us that the 62 richest people globally own more wealth than the bottom half of the world's population combined. The wealth of the world's 80 richest people doubled in five years to 2014.

By Prof. Muhammad Yunus, Nobel Laureate.
Co-founder of Yunus Social Business

THIS INFORMATION IS SO UNBELIEVABLE THAT IT TAKES TIME TO ABSORB. I feel like asking many more questions. How many of the world's richest people will own more wealth than is owned by the bottom half of the world's population, say, in 2025? It is obvious that if the number can drop from 388 persons to 62 persons in six years we are just one small step away from one lucky person owning more wealth than the entire bottom half of the world's population.

Concentration of wealth also means concentration of power – political and social – privileges and opportunities. The reverse is also true. If you don't have any wealth, you have no power, no privileges, no opportunities. The bottom 50% of the world's population, who own only a tiny fraction (1%) of global wealth, belong to this category. Tomorrow it will be worse.

Wealth concentration is an ongoing non-stop process which thrives under the present economic system. That's the point I am drawing your attention to: the richest people are not necessarily bad people (as popularly imagined) engineering the ever-expanding concentration of wealth with bad intentions. No, it is the system that does it for them.

Wealth is like a magnet. The bigger the magnet the greater its pulling force. It draws smaller magnets towards it. That's how the economic system is built. People with no magnet find it difficult to attract anything to them. If they somehow own some tiny magnets, retaining them becomes difficult for them. Bigger ones pull them to themselves. Unidirectional forces of concentration of wealth keep changing the shape of the wealth-pyramid, making its base thinner and its peak narrower and higher, ultimately looking like a thinning column rising out of a thin but large base.

Ultimately it's about reclaiming power for the people. And this can be done through social entrepreneurship. Currently there are not enough jobs for the people, so let's forget about jobs. A job is not the people's destiny; it's an old fashioned idea that is driving us mad. Jobs are a faulty idea and they should have been abandoned in the previous century. Human beings are simply not born to work for anyone else. We are born as human beings, and humans are go-getters and problem solvers. That's what we did when we came to this planet; we are gatherers and hunters – we are not jobseekers. When we were in our caves we were not sending job applications to anybody, we just took care of ourselves. Someone had the idea that we should be working for somebody and then jobs came along. But in the very fibre of our beings we are entrepreneurs.

We tell the entrepreneurs in Bangladesh every day, repeat to

'I'm not a job seeker. I'm a job creator'

yourself, 'I'm not a job seeker. I'm a job creator'. My mission in life is to create jobs. And how did I implement that? I created social business funds so that all young people can come to me with a business idea. We give them 100% of the money as angel investors. In return for the money we've given them, all they have to do is give back and create more jobs.

The current education system is geared to producing workers, but suppose we created an education system that creates entrepreneurs, so at the end of the education system, you don't come up with a mere certificate, you come up with a business plan? The education system should make students creative and encourage them to utilise their creative power to get things done: it should not be a stilted programme to train you to fall at somebody's feet and serve them for the rest of your life.

We need more angel investors

with a difference. We need to create more social entrepreneurs. If they are successful then they give the money back. It will not be the government that does this because historically the government is not very good at it. It would be any individual or any group of people that gives the entrepreneurs the money to do it as a loan, as an investment and so on.

I say to you: are you worried about employment? If you are interested, then here is the solution. Take five unemployed young people and turn them into employers. Social businesses recycle money, they don't use it up. Entrepreneurs create the demand and in the process, they become job creators.

Inside, everyone is an entrepreneur. That's why I am blaming the education system. Instead of the children being taught 'know thy self', they are being taught 'know thy boss'. 'What company am I going to work for? How will I please them? How will I apply to them?' Is this the life of a human being – to impress someone just so they get a few bucks? It's human slavery. Do the things you wanted to do.

The unemployed and the impoverished often say 'the financial system is not built for me, it's built for the people who have lots of money'. So, in Bangladesh I created a social business hub to alleviate the issue of start-up money. *We also connect our business owners to contacts and offer them advice. We do not abandon our investees. This is where we can bring the Golden Rule of compassion into the world*

of wealth and entrepreneurship and say if you want to have opportunities for yourself, create opportunities for others. We lend to those so that they can help themselves and then help others.

Currently the world is home to a lost generation of youth who may never secure a job. But they should also know that their life can be within their control through entrepreneurship.

What's more, the issues of resource depletion and global warming that are happening right now are linked to one very critical thing: human greed. The system is driven by people who want to make money, and they don't care what they do to the planet.

It's the wrong system where 1% owns 19% of the world's wealth, and tomorrow it will be worse. The rich are depleting our resources with abandon because they are too busy making money. Unless we go with fixing the fundamentals there will always be issues. For example, we can fix the water shortage problem but it would be fixed for just two days and would unfix very soon because the system just works that way.

We have to change the idea that the economy has to be driven by selfish interests. Human beings are not robots. The system should give them a choice: 'should I run a selfish business or a selfless business?' Personally, I believe in selfless capitalism: a combination of selfishness and selflessness. The present system restricts people because it only allows selfishness. That's why it's unstable and is only standing on one leg. The

economic system should give people the choice between 'selfish business' and 'selfless business', or a combination of both.

Business schools are barely discussing compassion. They should be teaching both schools of selflessness and selfishness, so the pupil can decide which one to feed more. It seems religion talks about compassion, so business doesn't want to talk about it. Why? Why do you divide it? Why are you one person in the office and then another person out of it? We are all one person. Why can't we be the same everywhere? The choice to be selfish or selfless is very important.

If all the world's wealth is going to end up in the hands of 1% of the population, the extinction of the earth will come soon unless we change the system. It is this generation that will decide this world's fate; there is no more time. They must choose the Golden Rule of compassion to ensure that wealth can be filtered downwards as well as upwards.

'IT'S THE WRONG SYSTEM WHERE 1% OWNS 19% OF THE WORLD'S WEALTH, AND TOMORROW IT WILL BE WORSE'

By Craig Kielburger,
Co-Founder of the
WE Movement

YOUNG AT HEART

NO PASSIVE BYSTANDERS.
Blinking in the bright sunlight, 22
children emerged from a dark, fetid
shed that had been their home and
prison. The building was a carpet
factory near Calcutta where they had
toiled as slaves. Chained to looms,
the children were fed just one meal
a day to keep them hungry and
awake so they could work longer.
As rescuers from the South Asian
Coalition on Child Servitude helped
them into a convoy of jeeps that
would take them home to families
they hadn't seen in months, even

years, the group broke into song:
"Free! We are free!"

It was 1996, and at age 13 I had
just participated in my first raid
to free child labourers in India. I
climbed into a jeep, and took a seat
beside an eight-year-old boy named
Munnilal. As we bumped along the
rough roads, I taught him how to
work my video camera. Munnilal
told me how men had come to
his village and lied to his parents,
saying that if he went with them,
he would get good schooling and
learn to make carpets to support the

family. But there was no school, no
support for his family, only beatings.
Munnilal's back was a mass of scars.

The tale was interrupted when
the convoy came to a shallow river.
While we watched from the bank,
the first jeep tried to cross, and got
stuck halfway. We all surged into
the chest-deep water and began to
push. Powered by a mob of heaving
children, the first vehicle was freed
from the river, and then the second.

As we piled back into the jeeps,
Munnilal looked at me, soaked to the
skin and shivering. Though he was no less

saturated in his tattered and oversized clothing, he reached out and offered me the blanket rescue workers had given him.

I declined. Tiny and malnourished, Munnilal had far greater need. Yet I have not forgotten that moment of incredible generosity. It embodies what the Golden Rule means to me: to reach out and offer aid and comfort to those in need, as I would wish to be comforted in similar circumstances.

Since I first heeded that call to help children around the world get the education and lives they deserve, I've seen a lot of progress on global issues like child labour. But the challenges are still huge.

As I write this, alarming reports are emerging from the Middle East. Child labour is skyrocketing among the hundreds of thousands of young Syrians in countries like Jordan and Turkey, who fled the carnage of civil war in their homeland. These children are working farm fields, cleaning houses, and even operating factory machinery to help support their desperate families. In Nigeria, the Islamic militia Boko Haram is kidnapping girls and turning them into suicide bombers. And in a remote northern indigenous community in Canada, poverty and hopelessness are fuelling an epidemic of youth suicides.

In a way, children are like the canary in the coal mine; their plight shows us where our world is taking a wrong turn. But the question is not: how can such things happen? Instead, it is: why aren't more people trying to do something about it? The Dalai Lama phrased the problem succinctly some years ago: "the greatest challenge facing our century is that we are raising a generation of passive bystanders."

I believe there are two fundamental reasons people don't heed the call to action embedded in the Golden Rule, refusing to act on the problems they see in the world. The first is a lack of connection to those in communities different from our own. Sadly, it's human nature for people to feel less connected to, or compelled to help, others when we don't see them as being like us. Even our reaction to the homeless on our own streets

becomes 'us' and 'them,' and the latter is somehow worthy of less. The second barrier is the feeling of powerlessness. There are so many problems in the world, it's easy to become overwhelmed. Even when we feel a connection, we ask: how can one individual possibly make a difference?

Those may seem like insurmountable challenges, but the solution is much simpler than you'd think. What we've discovered is that, as much as children shine a spotlight on the problems of the world, they are also the solution. Young people have the power to change the world when we teach them compassion, and how to live by the Golden Rule, through what I call "service learning".

The idea behind service learning is to educate children about local and global issues – from homelessness, to child labour, to climate change; first in the classroom, and then encouraging them to work together to tackle those issues through volunteering and activism.

The goal of service learning is to create a sense of connection between the youth and the world, to change their perspective from "us and them" to "we".

Here's a powerful example of what happens when you help children discover a connection with others around the world. In January 2016, Grade 7 and 8 students at North Ward elementary school, in the small Canadian town of Paris, Ontario, gathered around a computer for a Skype chat with Nena Aqlan and Bushra Al-Fusail, two Yemeni peace activists who had escaped the vicious civil war ravaging their homeland. The event was part of a service learning initiative by teacher-librarian, Katie Connors, who wanted to educate her students about global social justice issues.

The youth listened as Aqlan and Al-Fusail described their childhoods in Yemen. One told a story of drawing straws with her friends to see who would have to knock on the neighbour's door after they kicked their soccer ball over the fence into his yard. The Canadian kids were slack-jawed; this was a situation they had all experienced themselves. Suddenly, Yemenis were no longer strangers from a strange land, they were people just like us. Filled with that newfound sense of connection, the children were appalled as the two women went on to describe the horrors unfolding in their country: the indiscriminate

aerial bombings killing thousands; the shortages of food and water; the children deprived of an education. After the Skype call, Connors told us the quietest student in the class - the boy who never raised his hand – stood up, shaking with outrage; he demanded to know why Canada wasn't doing more to help the people of Yemen.

This outrage translated into action. The students wrote letters to the Prime Minister of Canada and to local politicians, asking them what they were doing about the Yemen crisis. They made posters and hung a banner at an inter-school basketball tournament to educate more students. They even launched a social media campaign with hashtags like #YemenMatters to raise awareness.

In 2014, social research firm Mission Measurement surveyed almost 1000 educators, and current and former students who had participated in Free The Children's classroom service learning program, called WE Schools. The survey found that young people who had been connected to the world through service learning were 1.3 time more likely to vote, twice as likely to volunteer, and nearly eight

'Young people have the power to change the world when we teach them compassion'

times more likely to start a campaign to address a social issue, compared to youths who had not been involved the educational program.

One in five alumni from these programs have gone on to launch their own non-profit or social enterprise. These are kids like 15-year-old Mackenzie Oliver. When she was just seven, Mackenzie started the 'I Love Me Club' to help youth boost their self-esteem, and encourage them to make a difference in their communities. Sheli-za Kassam, 18, founded an organisation called Children's Birthday Miracles in 2013. Her initiative throws birthday parties for underprivileged children around the world.

What's really incredible is the power of service learning to connect with, and instill compassion in, those who even society has given up on.

In the remote desert outside Los Angeles, California, lies the Challenger Memorial Youth Center – a juvenile prison. At any given time it is home to roughly 240 young male offenders, including hardened members of LA's most notorious street gangs.

Two years ago, education experts devised a new school curriculum for LA's juvenile justice system. The primary goal was to improve literacy skills among inmates, but the educators wanted to impart more than just reading and writing. "One of the pieces these kids were missing was empathy. We were looking to engage them in something outside

'IN CHANGING ONE WORD, EVERYTHING CHANGES'

themselves," Leslie Zoroya, Challenger's lead educator, told us.

Zoroya and her colleagues introduced a service learning unit on child soldiers. The inmates read A Long Way Gone (Sarah Crichton Books, 2008), the memoire of former teenage fighter, Ishmael Beah, in Sierra Leone. It was an eye-opener, especially for the gang members who could see a reflection of their own violent lives in the brutality experienced by young combatants in Africa. One former inmate said that the use of gang language and signs dropped significantly after students read the book. Before the service learning began, a former inmate told members of my

team that most of the young offenders avoided the education program whenever they could, preferring to hang out in the dormitory TV room. But when they were connected to a whole new world of issues, and people who were more like them than they'd ever realised, the teens became enthusiastic about classes.

Just like the students at North Ward after learning about Yemen, Challenger students dove into advocacy projects. They created posters and flyers to raise awareness about child soldiers among youth at non-prison schools in

LA, and wrote letters to local politicians pushing them to take action.

Has there been a lasting impact? The former inmate my team members spoke to told me that, within weeks of being released, he was volunteering for a community organisation as a mentor to other at-risk youths, and helping out at a local seniors' home. Having completed high school at Challenger, this young man was also enrolling in college to study psychology so that he could continue to help others.

When Mission Measurement conducted its survey, it also specifically looked at impacts on youth from marginalised, low-income communities who are at higher risk of problems like addiction and criminal activity. When these youths participate in WE Schools service learning programs, they are 1.5 times more likely to respect their teachers, 2.1 times more inclined to share opinions in class, and almost 9 times as likely to launch a campaign to address a social issue they're passionate about.

But what about that second barrier I talked about – the feeling of powerlessness? The daily headlines inundate us every day with a world of problems too heavy for even Atlas to bear. It's easy for people to feel despair, wondering how we as individuals could possibly make a difference. So how did a group of kids at a school in small-town Ontario come to believe they could impact a war half a world away? How could inmates in an LA prison think they might bring change to an issue as huge as child soldiers?

By encouraging young people to take on big issues as a group, service learning turns 'how can I make a difference' into 'how can we make a difference?' And in changing one word, everything changes.

If you know you are part of something larger, that everyone around you is united and working together, suddenly big problems aren't so big.

That's the philosophy behind Free The Children's WE Day events, bringing together more than 200,000 students in 15 stadiums across Canada, the USA and in the UK to celebrate volunteering and activism. Sitting in an arena, looking out over a sea of other youths, every student realises that they're not just an individual, they're part of a movement.

They feel powerful and inspired. And that's not just a surmise – studies bear it out. 84% of the young people surveyed by Mission Measurement who were involved in service learning and participated in WE Days said they know they can make a positive impact on society – not "believe they can," but "know they can."

Our world today is bogged down very much like the jeep in the river. It's mired in conflict, injustice, poverty, and environmental degradation. And the waters are rising. Standing on the bank are the children of the next generation. Will they remain passive bystanders, or will they leap in and be part of the solution?

Let's use service learning to make the Golden Rule a part of the core curriculum in every classroom, from kindergarten to high school. Let's raise young people to feel a connection and shared bond with others around the world, and to understand, that by working together, they can solve any problem.

'HOW CAN ONE INDIVIDUAL POSSIBLY MAKE A DIFFERENCE?'

COTTONING ON

We must name and shame countries responsible for modern slavery

By Dr. David Fleming, Director,
National Museums Liverpool

MILLIONS OF FILM-GOERS WATCH BIRTH OF A NATION, 12 YEARS A SLAVE or Django Unchained believing these images of slavery to be a thing of the past and totally unconnected to them.

But here is a simple test: check, as you read this, to see if you are wearing an item of cotton.

If you are, as is very likely, there is a simple conclusion. You too are complicit in the slave trade by supporting an industry that is based around children working in the fields, rather than going to school.

Putting children to work is among the more pernicious forms of slavery existing today. Denied education and therefore ill-equipped to escape the poverty trap, it en-snares so many in nations such as Afghanistan and India.

Cotton is a perfect example of a global industry that is heavily reliant on the use of child labour. It is well documented for driving the transatlantic slave trade to plantations in Louisiana and Mississippi. Yet, today, exploitation is still happening across the industry.

Across the world there are millions who, instead of attending school, provide cheap labour for harvesting cotton, carpet-weaving, brick-making and textiles. In the UK most of our cotton clothes are acquired from countries that still use child labour.

There are an estimated 46m people trapped in some form of slavery around the world, on a scale not known in history, despite slavery being outlawed by every country on the planet.

Over many years high street companies have been investigated, only to deny that there is a problem with their supply chains, and I have some sympathy for global conglomerates with their thousands and thousands of suppliers who struggle to track the practice through their supply chains.

That is why we must go to a mega-level of vocalisation – to name and shame countries into ending the slave trade.

Some of what we tolerate from our trading partners, including countries like Saudi Arabia or the United Arab Emirates is almost breathtaking. But it's failing to address these issues which is the crime of Western politicians, businesses and individuals.

I've spent time in Dubai watching those poor workers struggling in the blazing sun for next to nothing, and then be carted off back to their horrible accommodation in little trucks at night. Slavery is an enduring curse on humankind, but in the democracies of the West we are failing to speak out.

At least 18.4m slaves live in the world's most populous democracy, India, where Dalits exist at the bottom of the iniquitous Hindu caste system; while more than half of the people held in slavery worldwide live in one of five countries: India, China, Pakistan, Bangladesh, Uzbekistan.

The only way to get Indian politicians to change is by having an international dialogue and shaming them, by saying: "This is not a practice that is acceptable in the 21st century. Just because it dates back 700 years I'm not going to continue sticking up for it."

This is not an easy thing for Western politicians to do, particularly as some of the nations we need to target are those we wish to court economically.

Across the world the nations with the highest incidence of slavery per capita are North Korea, Qatar and Uzbekistan. Meanwhile, an estimated 50,000 North Koreans are also forcibly employed in foreign countries, mostly in China and Russia, according to an October 2015 report by the United Nations Special Rapporteur on Human Rights.

Other nations with high incidences of slavery per capita include Kazakhstan, Sudan, South Sudan, the Democratic Republic of Congo, and Ivory Coast. The list is a long and depressing one.

As illegal as slavery may be, legislation certainly does not prevent it, and in some states, such as Saudi Arabia, Qatar and the United Arab Emirates, people-trafficking for the purposes of forced labour is effectively legal. Shockingly, slavery is now deemed by the United Nations to be the third most lucrative criminal industry in the world, after drugs and arms trafficking.

While modern slavery may not exist in precisely the same fashion as it did in the ancient world, its modern manifestations are more widespread, every bit as dehumanising and even more despicable, bearing in mind the many centuries that have passed that are supposed to have led to an ever-greater awareness of what constitutes civilised, compassionate behaviour.

Modern slavery can look like forced labour; human trafficking; debt bondage; sex trafficking; domestic servitude; forced marriage. By their nature each breaks the Golden Rule and challenges us to consider how a modern world would look if these issues were overcome.

The United States Department of State has warned that many children are forcibly abducted and used as combatants. Others are made to work as porters, cooks, guards, servants, messengers, or spies. Young girls can be forced to marry or have sex with commanders and male combatants. Both male and female child soldiers are often sexually abused and are at high risk of contracting sexually transmitted diseases".

According to the United Nations, ISIS holds nearly 4,000 Iraqis, men and women as slaves, almost all of them Yazidis.

But contrary to popular opinion, it isn't a phenomenon exclusive to Africa, or Asia – slavery is found everywhere, including in wealthy western democracies, and in those nations that should be doing the most to prevent it.

The United States Central Intelligence Agency estimates 50,000 people, largely from Mexico and east Asia, are trafficked into or moved through the USA each year as sex slaves, domestic workers, and in the garment manufacturing and agricultural industries.

Among those at the forefront of the campaign has been Theresa May, who promised her government would "lead the way in defeating modern slavery". The Prime Minister set up a task force on the issue upon taking office and as Home Secretary brought in the Modern Slavery Act, the first legislation of its kind in Europe, to put slave masters behind bars.

The UK Government's concern that slavery is a chronic problem in modern society also saw it enact anti-slavery legislation last year.

But even in the UK, it is estimated that there are between 10,000 and 13,000 potential victims. The Modern Slavery Act 2015 includes two "substantive offences", human trafficking and slavery – servitude, and forced or compulsory labour. These offences frequently involve the confiscation of passports and mobile phones, leaving victims, often poor and vulnerable migrants, though many are UK nationals, with no hope of escape.

At the International Slavery Museum (ISM) in Liverpool, UK, we study slavery in all its guises, and provide educational materials to children from all over the UK. We also work with bodies like Anti-Slavery International, to illustrate what modern slavery can look like.

The causes of slavery are complex: poverty, the world's most deep-rooted social issue, is a constant. Weak or corrupt governments (such as those in Uzbekistan, Turkmenistan and North

Korea), unethical businesses, inadequate national and international laws relating to business and employment, and discrimination, all play their part.

Providing education for all would be a very good place to make progress in fighting the curse of slavery, especially if accompanied by genuine international action to reject goods produced by slave labour.

We must have transparency in supply chains, and this is by no means impossible. But we must also end the silence, and make far more noise, unwelcome though that will be to some governments and businesses. It is in an atmosphere of silence and complicity that slavery thrives.

We need stronger condemnation, and stronger, concerted action, from courageous political, business and religious leaders.

Like all evils, slavery has to be fought against, not tolerated or indulged, or denied because it makes money for someone powerful.

'WE NEED STRONGER CONDEMNATION, AND STRONGER, CONCERTED ACTION, FROM COURAGEOUS POLITICAL, BUSINESS AND RELIGIOUS LEADERS'

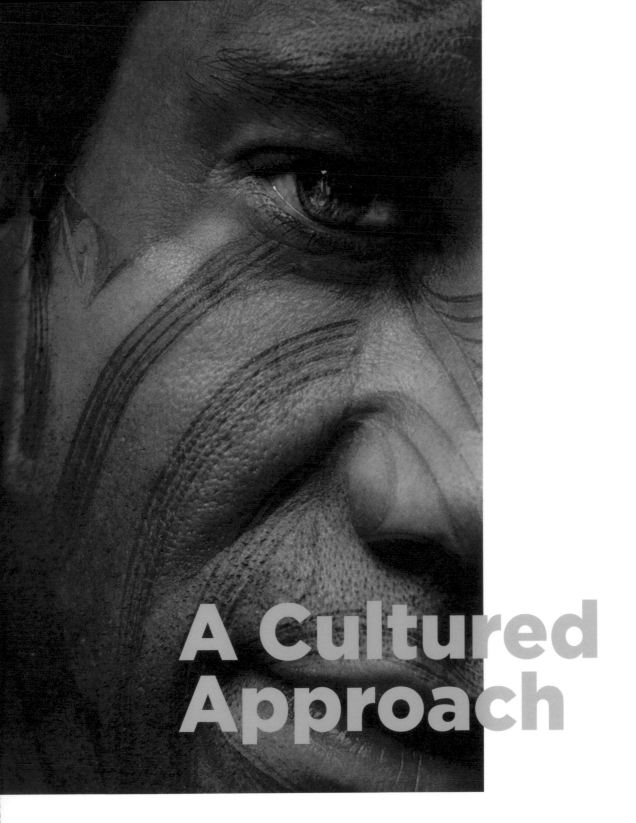

A Cultured Approach

An interview with Pauline Tangiora, Founding
member of the World Future Council

We need Western cultures to remember the Golden Rule and treat other cultures as they wish their own culture to be treated.

Were you conscious of wisdom being passed on to you growing up in a Maori culture?

Our elders didn't instruct us when we were children. We simply lived, and if we broke the rules, we were chided and guided into the right way of doing things which was the responsibility of the community.

Nuclear families are often too busy to help each other, but in a community you always have others to guide you. It's not about self, but togetherness. Maori people don't say, 'I did that' they say, 'We did it'. In the West, nuclear families tend to separate themselves in their own homes, but indigenous families cannot build a wall around themselves because they don't belong to themselves, they belong to the community.

What about your traditions of storytelling?

Storytelling is very important in Maori culture, especially around Matariki. (The Maori New Year signalled by the rising of the Seven Sisters constellation in late May, early June). When we see those stars together, it is our story time for our young.

Many of our children are named after their ancestors or the stars, and the stories we tell are part of our Whakapapa. (an oral tradition that explains how each individual is linked to their community and to the history of Maori culture). An example in another culture could be the story of the Scot, Robert the Bruce, who was inspired not to be beaten in battle after watching a spider trying to spin its web six times and falling down each time. We would describe that story as being part of the Scottish Whakapapa.

What can the West learn from indigenous cultures?

Perhaps other cultures cannot learn from indigenous cultures, but they can reawaken the same things within themselves, because in many non-indigenous communities everything is sleeping.

Spirituality is part of every human being's life, but you need to awaken that and say 'We have the same aspirations and ideas', and not be afraid to step out of your current way of doing things. Creativity does not belong to one indigenous group, it belongs to the Earth.

How do we reconnect with the Earth?

We reconnect with the Earth when we choose to seek the opportunities to be outdoors, to sit on the grass, walk the walks, be beside the rivers, and enjoy the land. Mother Earth is all embracing.

What have you learned from the indigenous communities you have met around the world?

Our community is very small, but some of us have been fortunate to meet with other indigenous communities with very different ways. Some are very much incorporated into Western culture, others are still living very much indigenously.

In Colombia the people in the mountains live a very traditional life, even though in the last couple of years they have had to come out to what they call 'the light'. They take their young men away into the darkness to learn the wisdom of their elders and their traditional values as they grow up. (The Kogi people of Colombia select certain male children from birth to live in a dark cave for the first nine years of

their lives and to tune into 'Aluna' described as: "A kind of cosmic consciousness that is the source of all life and intelligence and of the mind 'inside' nature").

How strong is Maori culture today?

In Maori culture, respect has to come from the heart, not through duty. For Maori, every hill, or stream, or river has some meaning in their culture and their language, and that is not always understood by Westerners in our country.

Certainly, Maori language is very much alive after coming close to disappearing entirely in New Zealand. Students are moving into Kura Kaupapa Maori (language immersion schools which also teach Maori values and principles) the Kohanga Reo (Maori language 'nests' for pre-schoolers) and post-graduate study groups.

All the things our young people are doing are very important, but they have also developed new environmental ideas that they have been able to put into practice. (The NZ Court of Appeal previously ruled the Maori language as a taonga, a treasure, to be protected.)

In Aotearoa (the Maori word for New Zealand) our traditional values are still very much alive on our marae (the meeting grounds and centre of the community for each Maori group). However, we live in two worlds and sometimes it is very difficult for the new generations. They need to follow the values of their community and the values of life and death, e.g. when somebody dies, the expectation is that families all return to the place they bring the body for the tangihanga (a Maori funeral rite where the deceased lies at the marae for three days surrounded by family and community, before taking the journey to his or her spiritual homeland). But many of our young people have jobs, making it very difficult for them to participate in the traditional values of our people.

How can we bring more compassion to the world?

We need Western cultures to remember the Golden Rule and treat other cultures as they wish their own culture to be treated. There also needs to be enough compassion in the world to allow people to live as they should. This is a question for the corporations who are buying up indigenous lands. Many indigenous people are nothing without their lands.

Has Western culture lost its spirituality?

It's wrong to say Western cultures don't have spirituality. Many people are starting to revive some of their Celtic spiritual values, which for indigenous people are very much part of our lives.

Maori culture is thriving and it makes me sad to meet other indigenous people who do not wish to move into a modern world.

It's also important to remember you cannot dominate people who are strong in their culture. A group of us went to the Earth Summit in Rio in 1992 as part of a small delegation and towards the end of the meeting, a man walked to the podium with bare feet. A few of those around the hall remarked: "Poor man he can't afford any shoes".

But, as we watched, he looked up and told us: "I don't need shoes to show that I'm a rich man. I walk and Mother Earth carries me". Everyone who was there remembers that moment still.

'There needs to be enough compassion in the world to allow people to live as they should'

* Pauline wishes to thank her niece Mary Wilson, who accompanies her on trips over-seas.

IN THE BEGINNING

Our people only counted as 'flora and fauna' until 50 years ago.

By Stella Wheildon, works to empower the ancient traditions of the Ngarakbal and their connection to all tribal nations of the earth

BEFORE THE INVASION AND OCCUPATION OF AUSTRALIA, the Aboriginal tribes, or as they prefer to be called, the Origine people, shared a cosmology and culture which metaphorically describes how 'sky heroes', or stars, created this beautiful planet for all of life to harmoniously share.

The Origine Elders knew that the stars created our precious earth and brought the sacred waters from the sky. They taught us that it is the role of the people to always remember their obligations to all 'skins' (or lifeforms) residing in the land, and to celebrate them through ritual, song and ceremony, while refreshing them at every djurebil (sacred site) to restore their natural balance.

For a people with a history officially traced back 45,000 years, it has always been lore for these rituals to be enacted in accordance with the galactic calendar of celestial orbits.

The purpose is to protect the earth and water and nurture our 'little relations', the animals, plants, fish, birds. Never forget, we are one, together, linked by the vast biological sea of water that flows through all life on this planet, no matter the species; we share the same water inside and though we have many 'skins', or forms, we are all related. We are all 'clever-water'.

Our first lore, 'Don't be Greedy', can be seen in the stars above our ancestral lands. (Others require groups to share everything and leave each place as it was found). The message is always, give thanks before you take and respect the importance of each and every life form in the eternal circle, just as it was in the eternal Dreamtime.

But it isn't like that now in Australia. Two separate government administrative systems exist, one for all Australians and one just for the Aboriginal peoples. The Aboriginal system is not representative of the Origine peoples, in fact colonisers decreed Australia was no man's land so they could take it without treaties, hence the designation of its people as 'flora and fauna'.

Later, an administrative system of created nations was implemented on a continent which once had moiety (skin) systems. This imported system fails to acknowledge that over 400 individual indigenous cultural blocks existed in Australia, everyone with its own land and language, every one unique.

The descendants of the survivors of those terrifying days have been shuffled and reshuffled until the uniqueness of their pre-invasion culture has been homogenised with every moiety across the continent, reclassified as all being 'Aborigines', for ease of administration.

Meanwhile entire groups of remnant survivors, living in mineral rich lands coveted by government backed corporations, are being forced to relocate yet again, resettled into centralised administrative areas, these dispossessed are refugees in their own continent.

Their fear and desperation propagandised to the world as them being 'dysfunctional aboriginals in need of administration' furthers

the apartheid system agenda. Such an agenda turns the people against each other to enable mining rights and exploitation of the ancestral land and waters they were only just allowed to reclaim and are now forced to abandon again.

It wasn't until 1967 when the Origine people were granted the legal right of being human by the Commonwealth, that they were allowed to return to their lands. Up until that time they had been collectively classified as flora and fauna and forced to live on centralised reserves where they had had no choice but to accept the same ignorance as our 'little relations' are subjected to today.

Since that time, a suite of aboriginal legislative governance was created and over the subsequent fifty years, legislative sleight of hand has stealthily amended those laws to exploit them.

Despite years of court cases to get back what rightfully belongs to them, the extinguishment clauses ensure that the land's title remains with the Australian government.

The Ancestral matristic lore (a system where females hold primary power) did not entertain the concept of separation or supremacy, everything was acknowledged as being interconnected. Man was not the superlative being. As with the Golden Rule, everything had its place, with all species afforded equal status on the tree of life.

The 'great tree of creation' spans our Milky Way, which is our eternal river of life. 'Illud Tempus' in Latin means 'time now' and also represents the atemporal telling of dreams, of unconscious time, just like our Origine Dreamtime.

Origine Lore, keepers understand that it is only the heart-intent of the keeper of the 'djurebil' which manifests the reality of matter, and despite the atrocities enacted on their homeland and their people, the love and compassion of the elders has never diminished. As a global village we can use this same vibration of love and forgiveness to renew our planet.

The earth was not created to be just a cultural topography for man alone, but one in which all nature shared in its significance, interacting in a way that does not attribute to either a supremacy or a primacy.

'THE EARTH WAS NOT CREATED TO BE JUST A CULTURAL TOPOGRAPHY FOR MAN ALONE, BUT ONE IN WHICH ALL NATURE SHARED IN ITS SIGNIFICANCE'

TOUCH THE JAGUAR

An interview with John Perkins, bestselling author of New
Confessions of an Economic Hitman, board member Dream
Change and The Pachamama Alliance

Is there a function for the Golden Rule in modern society?

I travel a great deal and what I find is people are all waking up to the fact that we live on a very fragile planet: a virtual space station; and it has no shuttles. We can't get off and it's headed for disaster.

Our conflicts with countries vying against one another and everybody working against Nature isn't working. We are all in this together and this idea of 'Doing unto others as they would do unto you,' is a useful way to counter that.

Are the tribes you visit prepared to adopt a different life as the world expands?

One of the groups I work with in the Amazon is the Achuar people who were uncontacted until the 1970s. They had not known the outside world, except for a few missionaries. Now it is essential for them to have two-way radios in order for them to keep oil companies off their land. They need to be able to communicate with each other, without having to run through the forest for two days to the next community.

Solar panels are being installed which help them to carry water, so the women don't break their backs by carrying it uphill from the river. There are a lot of things they want or can buy into.

They realise they can't live under glass and the outside world is becoming part of their culture. There are very, very few cultures that are untouched, apart from a few in parts of Indonesia and the Amazon; but most of the indigenous peoples know the only way they can protect themselves is by understanding us. They have an expression that says you must 'touch the jaguar'. You can't run away from the things that frighten you.

But the thing they don't want is a philosophy that is about taking everything that you can right now and not leaving it to their children, their grandchildren, and their great-grandchildren.

What is the current situation for the Achuar people?

They want to work closely with us, for instance, with the Pachamama Alliance, which was born out of an invitation they made for people to work in partnership internationally to preserve their land and culture, while bringing forth a new world view to honour and sustain life. We also help them to protect their forest. We pay for lawyers to legally keep the mining companies out of their territories. We have support programmes in 83 countries. But they also believe that they can help us move to a more objective reality.

What would that new reality be about?
Is progress illusory?

It depends on how you define progress. If you are living in the slums
of Calcutta or London or New York, you need housing and goods and
opportunities. We have to understand that roughly 3bn people are living
in very serious poverty and on the brink of starvation. Progress for them
means creating more food, better housing and more clothes.

But in the West, we are in a Death Economy. It is killing itself. It
is an economy that, to a very large degree, is based on warfare. There is a
terrific opportunity here for us to move to a whole new economic system
and that is happening. Costa Rica recently became the first country to
fully switch to renewable energy, meanwhile Aruba gets all of its water
from the ocean by desalinising sea water. Many countries we thought of as
being in the Third World, are really leading the way. We all need to buy
into that and encourage corporations to contribute to it, too.

Are the world's systems too large to change
fundamentally?

We have certainly got to hope not, because if we can't change, we can't
survive as a species on a planet that we can recognise. Any species that
has to discuss whether to be sustainable or not is in for trouble because if
you are not sustainable, what happens to you? You don't sustain.

Big business is globalised and of all the largest economies in
the world, many of the top 100 are corporations and they really control
the world now. In business school in the late 50s, I was taught that a
good CEO needs a decent rate of return, but is also a good citizen, who
considers the public interest and that's how the leaders of corporations
should run them. Give your employees a decent wage, give them
healthcare and pension funds and take great care of the communities
where you work.

All that changed in 1976 when Milton Friedman, who won the
Nobel Prize for Economics, said the only thing businesses should concern
themselves with is maximising profits, regardless of the social and
environmental costs. It created a huge change and in essence gave CEOs
the right, some would say the mandate, to do whatever it would take to
maximise profits, including corrupting politicians and destroying the very
resources upon which their businesses depend.

Back then financial capital was scarce and the Earth's resources
seemed abundant. We could pull out all the resources we needed
limitlessly and emit all the pollution we liked. The thing is nobody
believes that any more. It's a failed system and we need to change it.

You were once an 'economic hit man'; have you come to terms with the guilt you felt when working to undermine developing countries?

I came to understand that the only reason a system of economic hit men works is because the rest of us give it permission to exist. At best, we look the other way; at worst, we are ignorant of it, or actively support it. I used some of the bribes I took to create Dream Change and other organisations which helped to assuage my guilt.

One of the things that most bothered me was having to admit to myself that I had not only looked the other way but also had convinced many people to actively support that system, but I have since made a commitment to myself to be more diligent; to watch more closely what is going on in my community, my country, and the world.

So, what do we have to learn from other cultures?

Well, the biggest thing that industry can learn is that it's essential for each generation to turn over to the next generation a better world. In modern times, the last 100 years or so, we've interpreted a better world with more materialistic things: more money, bigger houses, more cars, but we are understanding now that that isn't a better world.

Are there ways the mainstream of society can hasten that change?

Yes, and for me it is, to a large degree, about changing corporations. Corporations run the world and we run corporations. We, the people. They wholly depend on us to buy their goods and services, to work for them, to invest in their stocks, to support them through government policies. It is totally dependent on us. The market is like a democracy, so one of the things I say, is pick a corporation that you want to change. Whatever that corporation is, if it's BP, Walmart, or Nike, then send an email to that corporation every week saying 'I love you, I love your products, but I'm not going to buy them anymore until you pay your workers a fair wage, or stop polluting the Amazon,' or whatever the issue is; and don't only send it to the corporation, but to all your social networking contacts, too, and get them to send it to all of theirs and then get everybody else to send an email as well. That has a huge impact. CEOs pay a lot of attention to what their customers are demanding.

Does it work?

Corporate executives are smart people and they want a world they can pass on to their children. A number of CEOs of big corporations tell me: "What I want is for my customers to write me hundreds of thousands of emails telling me I must change, so I can make those emails, or a summary of them, available to my top stockholders, and say 'Hey, we've got to listen to these people.'

Can the court of public opinion only hold them to account for a short time or change things wholesale?

Absolutely, they can change things wholesale. When I was in college there was apartheid in South Africa. We boycotted the products or organisations that supported it. We got rid of apartheid.

Parts of Europe and America were terribly polluted and we got corporations to clean them up. Since I was in business school, we've forced corporations to open their executive doors much wider to women and minorities. There is still progress to be made in all these areas, but we've made a lot of progress. We've got the corporations to label the number of calories, the number of proteins, the amount of sugars... we have had tremendous success. Just a small number of people can have a huge impact on corporations. We need to understand that.

Are indigenous nations confused about why we in the West live so unsustainably and have such a rapacious culture?

One of the things the communities I go to tell us constantly is that we have to change our dream of the world. This dream of consumerism and materialism is destroying us.

'This dream of consumerism and materialism is destroying us'

Ground Control

By Prof. Johan Rockström, Director of the Stockholm Resilience Centre

WELCOME TO THE ANTHROPOCENE

If we all take care of our planet's beauty, as you love and care for your dearest Nature, then humanity stands a good chance for a prosperous future on Earth. Give the planet your love and the planet will give you and your children all and more back. Safeguard the beauty of Nature for our own prosperity and future.

WE CANNOT ALL BE ASTRONAUTS...

It has been verified several times, that when astronauts, trained in scientific methodology and logical thinking, see Earth, the little beautiful blue marble ball, for the first time from space, it fundamentally changes their relationship to planet Earth, our only home. They see the green continental landmasses surrounded by blue oceans, and the blue varnish layer covering the entire surface, so thin that there are no paint brushes so fine to paint such a narrow layer in an artistic canvas view of Earth that constitutes our atmosphere. It is so thin, only 0.4-0.5% of the distance from the centre to the periphery, but is the holder of all life on Earth.

This planetary atronaut compassion, the deep insight that our small fragile planet, bursting with beauty and life, is a little dot in an infinite universe of a myriad of dead stars and planets, is no doubt, a fundamental source of compassion. This leads to a deep mind-shift, where we realise, once and for all, that our lives, our world, depend on us caring for our small, beautiful, and sensitive home – Earth. This is an important step, when a human being, like you and me, realises that our future depends entirely on our ability to safeguard the fragile, almost miraculously stable, conditions on Earth for the future of our World.

The problem? Well, we cannot all be astronauts. At least not soon. So we need to rely on science, our own insights and ethical rationality, and our fantasy and emotional heart, to create a necessary mind-shift towards the most important compassion of all, to safeguard our own home – planet Earth.

THE THREE DEEPEST SCIENTIFIC INSIGHTS

Science has made remarkable advancements over the past 50 years in its understanding of how the Earth system operates and how humans interact with and impact on it (REF Reid et al., Grand Challenges). We now recognise that Earth is a complex self-regulating system, where all 'parts' interact, the living biosphere, the atmosphere, the stratosphere, the hydrosphere, and the geosphere.

We now know, for example, that the living biosphere, including forests, grasslands, coral reefs, wetlands and living species, regulates the global climate by absorbing carbon and heat (over 50% of the CO_2 emitted by humans is taken up by forests, soils and oceans, and over 90% of the heat caused by us through greenhouse gas emissions is absorbed by the oceans). In essence, this means that everything counts, from phytoplankton to ice sheets, in regulating the state of the Planet.

With all this knowledge, science can now convey three fundamental insights, which together constitute a profound mind-shift in our relationship between us humans and the world, and our home planet Earth. They are: the Anthropocene, Earth tipping points, and the Holocene. Together, these three change our perspective and pathway to our future. Perhaps this is the compassionate equivalent of an astronaut planet experience.

THE ANTHROPOCENE

We have now, as humanity, become the largest driver of change at the planetary scale. So large, that we surpass, in pace and magnitude, the natural forces of nature that have determined Earth's cycles from ice-ages to inter-glaciers and shocks, and from volcanic eruptions, to mass extinctions of species.

Now, we live in the sixth mass extinction of species, the first to be caused by another species: us humans. We have transformed 40% of the land surface on planet Earth to agriculture and cities. We have emitted so much greenhouse gas from fossil-fuels, once stored in the Earth's crust for tens of millions of years, that we have raised global temperatures by 1°C in 150 years. Conditions on Earth have varied in the past, but never so fast as now.

We entered a new geological epoch, the Anthropocene, from around 1940-1950 (Anthropocene Review). Real world observations show that this is the moment of the "Great Acceleration" of human pressures on the planet. We shift gears and embark on a myriad of 'hockey stick' patterns of exponentially rising negative pressure on Earth. From CO_2 emissions, to overfishing, deforestation, chemical pollution, land degradation, and to loss of biodiversity, humans have had a colossal impact on the planet. Before the 1950s we had environmental challenges, yes, but in local pockets around the world. Today, the world as a whole is at the top of a multitude of exponentially rising global environmental change curves.

These pressures have now reached so far, that we are hitting the biophysical ceiling of the capacity of the planet to continue supporting humanity in a stable way (Rockström and Klum, the Human Quest).

TIPPING POINTS AND SURPRISE IS NORMAL

In the Anthropocene, we humans pose unprecedented pressure on all life-support systems on Earth, from local ecosystems to oceans, ice sheets and the atmosphere. The question remains though: how does Nature respond to these biophysical 'punches' from humans?

This is complex to predict in detail, but one thing is certain: planet Earth is not responding in the way we humans assumed. We built up our economic and social systems on the assumption that things change linearly, incrementally, and therefore in predictable ways that we can 'control'.

Instead, Earth's universal behaviour of biophysical responses seems to be a surprise. It has

'In the Anthropocene, we humans pose unprecedented pressure on all life-support systems on Earth'

tipping points that switch between different stable states for ecosystems. For example, a rainforest can cross a tipping point and become a savanna; a savanna can flip into desert; and a clear and alive lake can tip into a murky dead lake (SRC Regime Shift Database). The drama is that Earth's living biosphere, scaling from local ecosystems to large biomes like the Arctic and the Amazon, can only resist such abrupt tipping points for a finite amount of time.

We humans pollute, emit gases, degrade the planet, load it with nutrients, and dry out ecosystems. Nature can initially absorb these abuses and dampen their impacts, but at a certain point its systems become saturated, losing the capacity to adapt and deal with shocks and stresses. They reach a tipping point, shifting into completely new states that are irreversible over long periods of time.

What is it that determines whether Nature crosses a tipping point? It is a shift in feedback systems. Take Greenland, for example. Greenland is a large biome that we depend upon entirely for our future. It holds seven metres of global sea level rise, and so functions as a planetary 'cooling system'. Moreover, in being white, it reflects back some 80-90% of incoming heat from the sun back to space.

Without Greenland in a stable 'frozen ice' state, there is no harmony for humanity on Earth. But Greenland also has its own feedback system, two stable states – a frozen one and a melted one. In its frozen state, the only one we know, need and desire, it is white, which gives it a self-cooling feedback, by reflecting back heat to space (just as a white car is cooler). When Greenland starts to melt, as a result of our emissions of greenhouse gases, it happens at first slowly, linearly, as long as the feedback system is in place.

But then, abruptly, Greenland can shift from self-cooling to self-warming, if and when the entire surface of Greenland is melting, leading to a darker colour which absorbs more heat than it reflects back to space. Greenland crosses a tipping point that can irreversibly push it from a desired self-cooling state, to a nightmare self-warming state.

Nature can exist in more than one state, and can tip from one state to another abruptly and irreversibly when tipping points are crossed. The issue is that we humans depend on keeping the climate, oceans, forests, ice-sheets, wetlands, lakes, grasslands, in their original states. We depend on our large biomes, like the Arctic, Antarctica and the Amazon and Congo rainforests, for our collective future as humanity on Earth.

The good news is that we do not rely on science alone to help us define the guardrail within which we need to stay to avoid tipping points. We can define them ourselves. All we love in nature, all the qualities we have included in our culture, music, poetry and storytelling, are our own moral definitions of the state of the planet that can support humanity. Our best mental pictures, songs and stories of birds, flowers, trees, fish, of rainforests, lakes, wetlands and savannahs, are Golden Rules for preserving the biosphere in a desired state.

THE HOLOCENE, OUR GARDEN OF EDEN

We now know that the warm inter-glacial epoch we have had on Earth since the last Ice Age, which we learnt in school to call the Holocene, is the only state of the planet we know that can support the modern world as we know it.

The Holocene is remarkable, providing humanity with almost miraculous environmental stability on Earth. We have been modern humans on Earth for almost 100,000 years, so we know what brutal shifts mean. We have lived through the turmoil of Ice Ages and brutal swings between hot and cold. During the entirety of this turbulent pre-Holocene period, we were only a few million hunter gatherers on Earth, subject to abrupt climate shocks, with temperatures swinging back and forth by 5-10°C in as short a time as a decade. We had, in short, a rough time. During a cold spell in the Ice Age, some 75,000 years ago, freshwater was limited, as was food, and we were probably less than 15,000 fertile adults left on Earth. We were on the verge of extinction.

Then, 12,000 years ago we enter the Holocene. Before long we made our most important discovery of all time, more important than the steam-engine, internet, and aircraft combined. We become farmers! Agriculture, domesticating animals and plants, started simultaneously on several continents. We started cultivating maize, rice, teff, wheat, barley. Why? Not because of a "eureka" moment by one clever farmer, but because humans wanted risk management.

In the Holocene, the environment settles into a remarkable harmony. Seasons fall into place, spring, summer, autumn, winter, become predictable year after year. Rainy seasons become reliable, as do growing seasons. In simple terms, it becomes 'worth it' to grow food rather than chase food. We invent agriculture, some 8,000-9,000 years ago, and off we go on the civilisation journey we know so well, from the Mesopotamian irrigation civilisations, to the Egyptian, Greek, Roman, Mayan, Chinese and Modern civilisations.

It is all about compassion. What makes our modern civilisations possible – stable rainfall, ecosystems, and temperatures – are also what we love about nature. We have cultural, historic and emotional relations to everything we depend on, like the century-old Oak tree on the meadow, the Acacia tree in the centre of the savannah village, the rainforest or coral reef outside of our window, and this determines our ability to thrive and have good lives on Earth. Sure, the genetic diversity of much of our animals and plants has been around for millions of years. But it is not until the Holocene that nature, as we know it, as we love it, as we depend on it for our social and economic development, establishes itself: the Iguazu water falls, the magic Tonle Sap lake, the Himalayan mystical mountains.

The conclusion is as simple as it is dramatic. The Holocene is the only state of the planet that we know can support a world soon holding 9-10bn citizens, all with the same ethical rights to development. But we are in the Anthropocene, for the first time, just as we are conscious that the Holocene is the Garden of Eden. We understand it, just as we are threatening the stability of the entire Earth system, threatening to push the entire planet across tipping points, where Earth could irreversibly shift away from a stable and resilient state that can support humanity.

SOCIO-ECONOMIC TRENDS

EARTH SYSTEM TRENDS

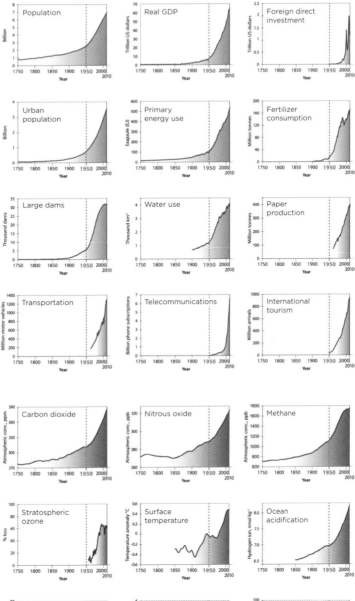

'Take care of the remaining beauty on Earth and we can ensure a good future for Humanity. But compassion cannot do it alone'

BIG WORLD, SMALL PLANET

When combining these new scientific insights, two deep mind-shifts occur.

The first is that we need to cross the mental tipping point, once and for all, that we have shifted, just over the past generation, from being a relatively small world on a big planet, to now being a relatively large world on a small planet. This changes everything. We have now reached a saturation point. We have filled up the entire environmental space on Earth. Continue pushing, filling the atmosphere with greenhouse gases, acidifying the oceans, transforming more than 50% of Earth's land surface, continuing the mass extinction of species, and we risk Earth tipping away from the Holocene state. This insight must shift our economy and our lives.

We have built our societies and economies on the assumption that Earth has an infinite ability to absorb our abuse.

We assume that Earth can subsidise our lives, while we fill nature on land with approximately 10bn tons of CO_2 and the oceans with another 10bn tonnes each year (half of our global emissions) at no cost. The world's largest subsidy to our economy. Normally, economists hate subsidies. But not when Earth subsidises. Really at no cost? No, potentially at infinite cost, for our survival.

It is, according to the latest science, only from around 1990 that we started to tip over to a big world on a small planet.

Now we fill up the entire atmosphere (we emit 350ppm of CO_2). It is only now that we see the first large-scale collapses of ecosystems and fisheries (e.g. the cod fisheries out of Newfoundland).

It is only now that we experience, at large scale, tipping points in lake systems due to eutrophication and over-fishing. It is only now that we truly threaten, for the first time, a planetary catastrophe, due to the depletion of the stratospheric ozone layer.

Yes, we entered the Anthropocene in the 1940s-1950s, but evidence indicates clearly, that up until roughly 1990, Earth seemed to have had the resilience to cope with this escalated pressure, hiding our abuse.

COMPASSION

It is only in the past 25 years, that we have started seeing signs of hitting the ceiling of planetary capacity to support humanity in harmony.

A new human Earth compassion must enter centre stage. A compassion that translates to a simple rule of life; take care of the remaining beauty on Earth and we can ensure a good future for Humanity. But compassion cannot do it alone.

The world needs decisive leadership to guide rapid change, e.g., towards decarbonisation of the world's energy systems and towards sustainable agriculture that causes no further loss of species, deforestation or eutrophication.

It is at a very promising juncture with rapid growth of sustainable technologies and systems, from cheap and effective solar energy systems, to sustainable and healthy food systems, that can generate better lives for all.

Clearly, we need to admit that we live in a world with islands of insights in an ocean of ignorance. But the archipelago of islands is getting denser.

Universal compassion can be the critical factor tipping the world over into a new logic, that world prosperity can only occur within Earth's planetary boundaries. We can only succeed if avoiding potential catastrophic risk and mainstreaming global sustainability becomes the 'only' logic for all investments, technologies, urban planning schemes, infrastructure projects and household behaviour. Unsustainable development, our route so far, is a dead end.

It is possible; we have a universal red thread that we all, as citizens on Earth, share. We know what we love in our closest environment... the Acacia tree outside of the mud hut in Niger, the coral reef outside of the Raja Ampat fishing villages, the Ice Age polished granite rocks in the Swedish archipelago. We all have a relation to Nature. Global sustainability, in essence, is to reconnect our human wellbeing and progress to nature, i.e., to reconnect with what we love.

'Our relationship to nature may be a "collective unconsciousness", undeveloped as a global force, a Golden Rule for humanity'

CREATING CHANGE

Could it be that such an underlying and deeply ingrained relationship with nature, among all human beings, is the key to unlocking a rapid global transformation to a sustainable future?

Psychiatrist Carl Jung's early 20th century theory of "collective unconsciousness" was that all individuals have an inherited consciousness, which forms "archetypes" of universal and collective underlying rules of human behaviour (Ref Jung). Our relationship to nature may be a "collective unconsciousness", undeveloped as a global force, a Golden Rule for humanity, in the same vein as the Golden Rule in most religions and cultures.

There is most likely a universal underlying common human denominator among us all. We all have a relationship with beauty on our planet – be it a shanty town dweller in Nairobi's Kibera slums, or a 55th floor apartment in urbanite New York. This could be our 'collective unconsciousness', the red thread that unconsciously runs through all human beings, bringing a shared love of our freshwater, clean air, the smell of exploding flowers in spring, the sweet savannah smell after rainfall.

PARETO THEORY

If we have collective unconsciousness, as Jung suggests; and we have a Golden Rule, then, across the world, religions and cultures, we have a common unconscious support for safeguarding Earth within planetary boundaries! But, given the planetary urgency for humanity, how do we mobilise this compassion?

If we combine this collective unconscious support with the ethical Golden Rule of not doing unto others that which you would not do unto yourself (e.g., emitting greenhouse gases or polluting water), then the rising evidence is that large minorities of engaged, innovative thinkers and solution holders can tip behaviours, markets, and perspectives at a grand scale.

This follows the old theory of the 19th Century Italian economist Vilfredo Pareto and the 'Golden Rule' of how to cross the valley of death in innovation business development; that a large enough minority penetration of a market can tip over an ignorant majority or mainstream a solution.

When a vanguard reaches up to approximately 20% it can tip over the business sector, behaviour, perspectives, and shift the majority.

This applies to mobile phones, to travelling, and the internet. It is never just a majority that shifts behaviour. It is a large enough minority.

We have an opportunity to awaken a collective and unconscious love for Earth. The 'Golden Rule' can safeguard Earth's beauty for our own prosperity. It can help the large minority manifesting compassion, morality, and innovation (the 'David') to overcome the 'silent majority' ('The Goliath').

Despite the scientific reasons for despair over rising global environmental risks, there is reason for hope. The world's political leadership has finally recognised that people only thrive if our planet is kept intact. The exponential rise in sustainable solutions is gathering momentum every day, through sustainable decarbonisation, digitalisation, nano-technological break-throughs, and more.

Combine that revolution, a minority Pareto moment, with an awakened collective unconsciousness, and we may have a global transformation to a sustainable future for humanity. An 'Astronaut moment' for all!

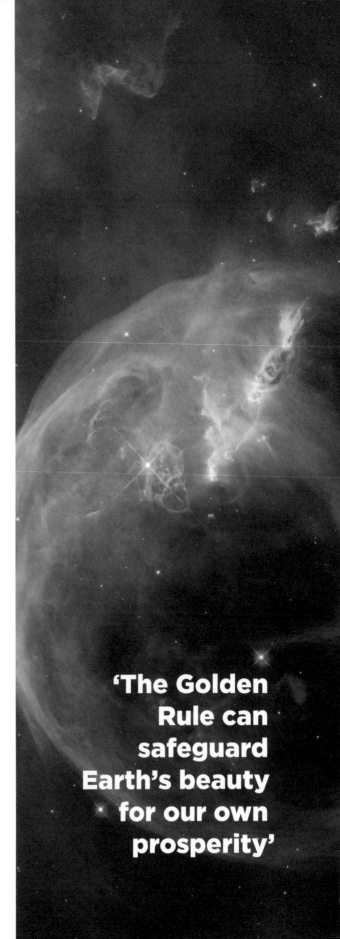

'The Golden Rule can safeguard Earth's beauty for our own prosperity'

NINE

THE

By Prof. Johan Rockström, Director of the Stockholm Resilience Centre

PLANETARY

BOUNDARIES

IMAGINAL CELLS: VISIONS OF TRANSFORMATION | THE NINE PLANETARY BOUNDARIES

143

We must acknowledge the new predicament for humanity on Earth. The evidence of our move from the Holocene (which started about 10,000 BCE) to the Anthropocene (current human-dominated period) and Earth's tipping points lead to the necessity of answering two fundamental questions:

1 What are the biophysical processes that regulate the stability and resilience of Earth? Or, what will it take for our Home to remain in a Garden of Eden-like state?

2 If we can identify the processes in (1), can we rely on science to provide us with quantitative boundaries, beyond which we risk crossing tipping points that can irreversibly push us away from the Holocene, but which, if we stay within them, provide humanity with a safe operating space on Earth for world development?

SCIENCE HAS DEFINED THESE AS PLANETARY BOUNDARIES

In 2009, a group of Earth system scientists identified the nine planetary boundary processes that regulate the stability of our planet (Rockström et al., 2009). Six years later in 2015, another conclusion (Steffen et al., 2015) was both reassuring and sharper. If we as humanity can become sustainable stewards of the nine planetary boundaries, we stand a good chance of safeguarding a stable planet for future generations.

These nine can be grouped in three logical clusters. The "Big Three" include: (1) preserving the global climate system by limiting global warming to under 1.5°C; (2) keeping the protective Ozone layer intact in the stratosphere; and (3) enabling stable oceans by avoiding deep acidification effects. These operate at the global scale, directly impacting planetary processes.

Then, we have the four "Slow Biosphere Boundaries", which operate at a smaller scale, but which provide Earth with its resilience; to dampen, buffer, adapt and be "strong" in the face of shocks and stress. These include: (4) biosphere integrity, to safeguard our richness of species on Earth and their ecological functions in seascapes and landscapes; (5) maintain a minimum of critical biomes on land, keeping the remaining rainforests, temperate and boreal forests intact; (6) assure the wettening of our landscapes by safeguarding the global hydrological cycle, i.e., not allowing water scarcity to knock over nature; and finally (7) keeping our human manipulation of the global nitrogen and phosphorus cycles within safe boundaries. These four each provide Earth's capacity to adapt and persist in our Garden of Eden state.

Then, finally, we have the two "Alien" boundaries, which are totally created by us and are not naturally occurring on the planet, including: (8) what we call novel entities, i.e., all chemical, nuclear, plastic etc., compounds that we allow to accumulate in the biosphere with knock-on effects we do not yet fully understand; and finally, (9) aerosol loading, i.e., the pollution of air, through black carbon, soot, sulfates, nitrates and other large particulates that create, for example, smog, at regional scales that can have dramatic knock-on effects on climate, rainfall, and human health.

In the latest assessment, the scientific conclusion is that humanity has already transgressed 4 out of 9 planetary boundaries (Figure 1). We are in a danger zone (in yellow) for climate change and land system change, and in a high-risk zone for irreversible tipping points for biodiversity loss and interference with the global nitrogen and phosphorus cycles.

It is logical that humanity needs to respect the biophysical processes that regulate Earth's ability to support humans. It is also clear that there must be certain points in nature, when pressure accumulates to a breaking point, when the "branch snaps".

'We remain a small world on a big planet'

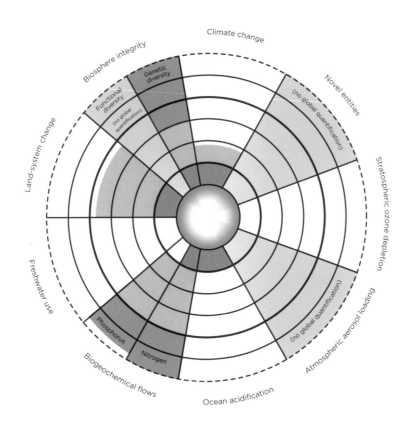

- Beyond zone of uncertainty (high risk)
- In zone of uncertainty (increasing risk)
- Below boundary (safe)
- Boundary not yet quantified

Figure 1. *Planetary Boundaries, a safe operating space for humanity*

Source: *Steffen et al. Planetary Boundaries: Guiding human development on a changing planet, Science, 16 January 2015*

'It is a transformation
at a pace that
surpasses a
revolution within the
framework of the
Golden Rule'

We neglect it, believing that perhaps, after all, we remain a small world on a big planet. But planetary boundaries science, drawing on climate science (IPCC etc.), biodiversity science (UN MEA, IPBES etc.), hydrology, ocean science, stratosphere research, etc., is clear. We are now hitting hard-wired and non-negotiable processes that threaten to shift from being Eden-friend to Eden foes. Science thus verifies what may be an underlying belief that Nature, and ultimately planet Earth, has absolute boundaries.

We have not had this verified with scientific evidence until recently, thanks to the remarkable advancement in Earth system science over the past 30 years. We have not had the convincing proof that, yes, beyond 1.5°C global warming compared to the pre-industrial average, we risk crossing catastrophic and irreversible tipping points. But now we know.

In fact, we know that Earth is a complex self-regulating system with hard-wired inbuilt processes.

Earth behaves like our human body. We have learnt, through millennia that we too, as humans, have multiple stable states, and that body temperature regulates one tipping point between them. We know that at approximately 42°C, we abruptly shift from one desired state, that we are alive, to an undesired state, that we die. This biophysical body tipping point is complex, and is a result of interactions and feedbacks between our body organs, immune system and blood flows, but still aggregates to a clear human boundary.

The same goes with the planet. Earth has her "42°C" equivalents, hard-wired in her biophysical interactions between organs – biosphere, atmosphere, geosphere and blood stream flows – the hydrological, carbon, nitrogen and phosphorus cycles. The trick is that we cannot interview Mother Earth and ask her where the tipping points are exactly. But they are there. Today we have come close; we have been able to define the nine planetary boundaries that determine the stability of the Earth system.

THE DRAMA OF TRANSFORMATIVE CHANGE

The dilemma is that we have come to the realisation late in the day of being a "big world on a small planet". Manifestations of these insights are now clear for everyone to see and act upon. In 2015, world leaders adopted the Sustainable Development Goals, which set a clear road map for people and the planet, for the first time in human history.

The goals include; eradicating poverty and hunger, ensuring equity, education, health and democracy, building partnerships and transparent institutions, all to be accomplished by 2030, for a world population that will inevitably grow to approximately 10bn co-citizens by 2050, for a world economy projected to grow by a factor of three. All this is to be accomplished within planetary boundaries. We now have concrete global goals for climate change (to stay as far under 2°C as possible),

oceans, freshwater, and biodiversity, set within the necessity of sustainable agriculture, and sustainable consumption and production, which defacto means a transformation to world development within planetary boundaries.

The Paris Climate Agreement in 2015 was a recognition that humanity's chance for future development is within a finite planetary boundary ceiling for climate.

Most polls show that approximately 70% of citizens worldwide are worried about climate change and want action. Business leaders – from the oil industry, to the car industry, and the food industry – see the rapidly rising risks, as well as the emerging technologies that make a transition to global sustainability possible, along with the sustainable benefits of better health, better well-being, and better democracy that does not threaten bottom-line profit or socio-economic development.

But have we woken up too late? The world is now on the biophysical edge. We need to bend the global curves of greenhouse gas emissions and degradation of our environment, within five years; we need to move along an unprecedented acceleration path, in order to reduce global emissions annually at over 5% per year.

This is massive. 195 nations, tens of thousands of multinational corporations, over 7bn people, all "singing the same song", playing in the same symphony, talking the same talk, moving towards a decarbonised sustainable world within planetary boundaries. It is a transformation at a pace that surpasses a revolution within the framework of the Golden Rule.

But we can only succeed if we combine rapid immediate action with a change in our relationship with Earth.

AMAZING GRACE

By Bishop Marcelo Sánchez Sorondo, Chancellor of the Pontifical
Academy of Sciences at the Vatican

'POTENTIA' INTO 'ACTA'. I am delighted to have the opportunity to contribute to this Imaginal Cells journal. As a Catholic Bishop serving for nearly 20 years at the Pontifical Academies of Sciences and of Social Sciences, it is only natural that I will frame my reflection as a Christian philosopher, though much of what I am going to say should hopefully speak to all people, irrespective of personal religious identification.

The German philosopher Heidegger coined the celebrated phrase that human beings were "thrown" into the world. But we are not called to live individually. Rather, human beings are called into existence to become truly themselves only when they are in relation to others, and of course, in its highest expression, to the Other that is God.

I therefore suggest that one great starting point in working towards making the world a better place is to be found in drawing attention to this fact, and in the building up of what might be called an inter-personal, inter-relational capital throughout society.

The idea is not that we should be filled with sympathy for others, with warm fuzzy sentiments, and then we carry on doing exactly what we were doing before. Rather, I think the idea is that we are then driven by these emotional responses, that we don't rest at simply being a potential neighbour to a stranger robbed and abandoned, left to die by the side of the Road to Jericho; but that we actually, moved by compassion, are motivated to do something. That is, to borrow from the Aristotelian terminology, that we move from potentia into acta!

So, when we are thus driven in our compassion by the sufferings of another, how should we govern our response? This is the central question to which I will return.

The three texts that I have chosen to act as a foundation for my proposal towards building a more compassionate society all come from the Gospel – the "Golden Rule", "the Beatitudes" and "Matthew 25".

The most perfect model of how to respond, I think, is summarised by what is popularly known as the Golden Rule: "do to others as you would have them do to you." [Lk 6:31]. Most religions have their own variant of this principle.

However, it is clear that a society where individuals genuinely wanted to receive nothing from others, would also, coherently, offer nothing in return! Or at the other end of the spectrum, a society where people genuinely wanted to give everything to others would also, again entirely coherently, expect to receive everything in return. Both are equally consistent applications of the Golden Rule.

Therefore, in order to complete the Golden Rule, the Beatitudes and Matthew 25 round off the evangelical exposition on compassion.

In the same way that the French philosopher Paul Ricœur spoke of the other as another self, Christianity has something unique to offer regarding the fullest interpretation of the Golden Rule.

The Danish Lutheran philosopher Søren Kierkegaard developed his concept of the 'moment'; that is, the precise moment when God gives a person a certain grace (for knowledge of God, conversion, repentance, etc.) that precedes an interior change of disposition. Whether or not this grace is accepted or rejected depends on the person, as it is governed by their freewill.

Let's apply Kierkegaard's insight into one of the most well-known and well-loved parables in the Gospel.

Jesus replied, "a man fell victim to robbers as he went down from Jerusalem to Jericho. They stripped and beat him and went off leaving him half dead. A priest happened to be going down that road, but when he saw him, he passed by on the opposite side. Likewise, a Levite came to the place, and when he saw him, he passed by on the opposite side. But a Samaritan traveler who came upon him was moved with compassion at the sight. He approached the victim, poured oil and wine over his wounds and bandaged them. Then he lifted him up on to his own animal, took him to an inn and cared for him. The next day he took out two silver coins and gave them to the innkeeper with the instruction, 'take care of him. If you spend more than what I have given you, I shall repay you on my way back'. Which of these three, in your opinion, was neighbour to the robbers' victim?" He answered, "the one who treated him with mercy." Jesus said to him, "go and do likewise." [Lk 10: 30-37]

Conventional thinking would suggest that the Good Samaritan was the benefactor, and the stranger the recipient, and of course, this is certainly true. But I do not think this is the total picture. In fact, a profoundly Christian reading of the parable reveals that on another, higher, meta-level, there is something else taking place.

This is the presence of another transfer that goes in the opposite direction; I believe an appreciation of this dynamic is crucially important

Benefactor $\longrightarrow$ **Recipient**
Good Samaritan, giving money, time, care $\longrightarrow$ **Victim**

but very rarely given sufficient attention. This is the insight that the robbed victim is himself a donor of something essential! He gives to the Samaritan the opportunity to be merciful, to be compassionate. He is the means by which the Samaritan can be the recipient of the Kierkegaardian moment.

It becomes an interesting question, then, who of the two actually gives the gift of greater value? Let me give one concrete example of this, that I personally experienced recently. In July of this year, I was invited to participate at the re-opening of the Carcer Tullianum, the three-millennia old prison in Rome that once held Saints Peter and Paul.

Benefactor $\longrightarrow$ **Recipient**
Victim, giving transfer of grace $\longrightarrow$ **Good Samaritan**

In amongst all the grand speeches of the assembled cardinals, politicians, architects etc., there was naturally also an opportunity given to the principle benefactor of the restoration. I was struck by what he said. He spoke with great sincerity, without notes, and simply thanked the organisers for having given him the opportunity to be generous towards such a worthy project. A benefactor thanked the recipient for having given him the opportunity to give! This is really counter-intuitive for the values of our contemporary culture, and it illustrates perfectly the point that I want to demonstrate.

It is this insight, I think, that lies at the heart of Pope Francis's mission; this is what he wants the Church to understand so much more profoundly. What I want to underline is the fact that in seeing our neighbour fallen on hard times, and in responding with compassion, we ourselves may become the willing recipients of a grace.

A radically Christian interpretation of compassion helps us therefore to see that when giving, through the action of Divine Grace, we ourselves become the recipients of a gift far more valuable. The Golden Rule finds its echo in the formulation "love one's neighbour as one's self".

This is at the heart of the New Testament: "teacher, which is the great commandment in the law?" Jesus said to him, "you shall love the Lord your God with all your heart, with all your soul, and with all your mind". This is the first and greatest commandment. And the second is like it: 'you shall love your neighbour as yourself'. On these two commandments hang all the Law and the Prophets".

[Mt 22:36-40]

What does the Gospel have to add? Can it perfect in a Christian way, an already perfect formulation? The most influential manifesto in all politico-religious language, the most revolutionary discourse, the most relevant, the most human and the most divine, the shortest and the most profound, that any man has ever pronounced during the course of human history, is that of Jesus's Sermon on the Mount. He went up on a mountain, and when He was seated, His disciples came to Him. Then He opened His mouth and taught them, saying:

"Blessed are the poor in spirit,
    For theirs is the Kingdom of Heaven.
 Blessed are those who mourn,
    For they shall be comforted.
Blessed are the meek,
    For they shall inherit the Earth.
Blessed are those who hunger and thirst for righteousness,
    For they shall be filled.
Blessed are the merciful,
    For they shall obtain mercy.
Blessed are the pure in heart,
    For they shall see God.
Blessed are the peacemakers,
    For they shall be called sons of God.
Blessed are those who are persecuted for righteousness' sake,
    For theirs is the Kingdom of Heaven.
Blessed are you when they revile and persecute you, and say all kinds of evil against you falsely for My sake."

I add to the Beatitudes, Matthew 25: 31-46, because in consideration of compassion, the two texts complement one another so well.

By performing acts of mercy, one works towards one's own salvation. St Augustine claims that we all sin in this world, but not all of us condemn ourselves: those who do penance and perform acts of mercy are saved.

In essential terms the Beatitudes and Matthew 25: 31-46 are more concrete existentially than the Golden Rule, which is always maintained through an abstract view of the other. These two texts, on the other hand, which speak about the other in his existential situation of suffering, demonstrate concrete suffering and its correspondent compassion that is not present in the Golden Rule.

Unlike the Golden Rule, in the Beatitudes and Matthew 25: 31-46, suffering is not only defined as physical suffering, as mental or moral pain, but also by the diminution or the destruction of the capacity to be and to act, to be and to be able to do, which are felt as an attack on the integrity of the dignity of the person.

Tying all these themes together, then, from the point of view of the eternal, the Holy Gospel has something essential, something absolutely mind blowing, to teach us about the under-appreciated gift that is compassion.

The point is not to apply the Golden Rule motivated only by a kind of karmic optimism, being good to others so that others may be good to us: the Golden Rule remains the perfect rule for teasing out of the conscience, which tends to selfishness, what the correct moral comportment might be.

In conclusion, then, I hope my outline of these three texts taken together illustrate just how inexhaustibly profound the concept of compassion is, and how the Gospel always has something essential to teach us in every age in the challenge of building a more compassionate society.

Personally, I think that our society would lose a lot of its nervousness and tension if we were able to internalise the realisation that the recipient of charity is also a benefactor. Blessed are those who in the contemporary world are capable of creating a more compassionate society.

'THE MOST PERFECT MODEL OF HOW TO RESPOND, I THINK, IS SUMMARISED BY WHAT IS POPULARLY KNOWN AS THE GOLDEN RULE: "DO TO OTHERS AS YOU WOULD HAVE THEM DO TO YOU" [LK 6:31]'

A Balancing Act

"Is that nice? "If it's not nice, is it necessary? "Would you like to hear the same words addressed to you by another?". The wisdom of the ages encapsulated in the three questions that my mother addressed to me. They so often prompted me to bite my tongue, but they were a very practical application of the Golden Rule." Mpho Tutu van Furth

By Archbishop Emeritus Desmond Tutu, Global activist for peace, democracy and human rights and Nobel Laureate and Mpho Tutu van Furth, Director, Tutu Institute for Prayer and Pilgrimage

OUR CAPACITY TO RECOGNISE OUR INTERDEPENDENCE HAS BECOME FUNDAMENTAL TO OUR SURVIVAL AS A SPECIES ON EARTH. We now know, through various studies, that while gross domestic product has increased in the West in recent decades, happiness has not.

So, we cannot worship money and our self-interest alone. It leaves us with a hunger that can never be satisfied by acquiring more goods.

What matters more is that we understand how we should behave to one another: namely, following the Golden Rule, that we should treat others as we would have others treat us.

All major religions have love and compassion at their core, promote tolerance not violence and hate, and most have their own version of the Golden Rule – treat others as you wish to be treated. They all recognise that human happiness ultimately comes from our relationship with each other.

Our capacity to relate to others and to recognise our interdependence is more urgently needed than ever when it comes to peace, prosperity and saving our beautiful environment. It has become fundamental to our survival as a species on earth.

We can truly only survive together. We have enough evidence of the devastating effect of not doing so: wars, violence, high security fencing, environmental degradation, global warming, malnutrition and child poverty even in the richest of nations.

Most human suffering is man-made, so let's see the opportunity in this and work together to create solutions that unite us; build bridges of understanding, oppose negative rhetoric, stand up against hatred and injustices, support human rights and equal opportunities, and soften the blow for those hardest hit by economic crises.

We also have to be better at stemming the abuses of the modern world, from environmental decline to corporate malpractice, to the abuse of workers in supply chains for goods that we all love to own.

In the same way, shareholder responsibility is not only to make profits; it is also how they are made that matters. We should demand transparency and

be opposed to highly leveraged products that do not actually produce anything useful for the common good.

Does this mean we should not enjoy all earth's goods and riches? No. Enjoy them. Earn them. It is a misconception that one has to be poor to be spiritual, and that hard work should not be rewarded. What is important is finding the balance between greed and having enough, and defining what a joyful life means to us.

We can earn a living through capitalism, not by profiteering but by genuinely serving others. Even in the process of producing a profit, we can put the Golden Rule at the heart of our society: we can do no harm and make the world a better and fairer place.

In using the Golden Rule at the heart of our society we can make the world a better and fairer place.

'We can truly only survive together'

PETER BAKKER
("Green Money", p. 52)

Current Role: President and CEO, World Business Council for Sustainable Development.
Education: HTS Alkmaar; Erasmus University, Rotterdam, (NED).
Career Snapshot: Former CEO of TNT NV. Recipient of Clinton Global Citizen Award 2009 and 2010 SAM Sustainability Leadership Award. UN World Food Programme Ambassador Against Hunger. Chairman, War Child, Netherlands.

JANE CORBETT
("Hearts & Minds", p. 24)

Current Role: Founder: Generative Leadership Centre (Oxford) and associate at Future Considerations and Mobius Executive Leadership.
Education: B.A. University of Cambridge and University of Oxford – MPhil Economics, (UK).
Career Snapshot: Leadership and innovation facilitator, trainer and coach. Has designed and directed programmes at the University of Oxford, Cambridge Institute for Sustainability Leadership, Lead International, Warwick Manufacturing Group and corporate partnerships with Earthwatch Europe.

DR. DAVID FLEMING
("Cottoning On", p. 116)

Current Role: Director, National Museums, Liverpool.
Education: Leicester University, (UK).
Career Snapshot: Founder and creator of the Yorkshire Museum of Farming. Principal keeper at Hull Museums. Director of Tyne and Wear Museums. Past President of the UK Museums Association, he has served on several Government committees and task forces. Awarded an OBE for services to museums. President of the Federation of International Human Rights Museums.

VICE PRESIDENT AL GORE
("Home Truths", p. 10)

Current Role: Founder and chair of Generation Investment Management and the Alliance for Climate Protection. A member of the Board of Directors of Apple Inc., a senior adviser to Google and a partner in venture capital firm Kleiner Perkins Caufield & Byers.
Education: Graduated Harvard A.B. cum laude and attended Vanderbilt University Law School (USA) before running for political office.
Career Snapshot: An elected official for 24 years, he served as Congressman and Senator for Tennessee before becoming the 45th Vice President of the United States from 1993 to 2001. The subject of the 2007 Academy Award winning documentary, An Inconvenient Truth, and the joint winner of the 2007 Nobel Peace with the IPCC for his work on climate change.

DR MOHAMMED "MO" IBRAHIM
("One Dollar", p. 88)

Current Role: Sudanese-British mobile communications entrepreneur. Founding chairman of Satya Capital Ltd, a private equity fund focussed on Africa and chairman of TPG-Satya, a joint African investment alliance. Founder and Chairman of the Mo Ibrahim Foundation.

Education: BSc in Electrical Engineering from Alexandria University (EGY) Master's degree in Electronics and Electrical Engineering from University of Bradford. PhD in Mobile Communications from the University of Birmingham, (UK).

Career Snapshot: Founded Celtel after working for British Telecommunications, building up 24 million mobile phone subscribers in 14 African countries. After selling the company for $3.4 billion, he set up the Mo Ibrahim Foundation to focus on the critical importance of governance and leadership in Africa through four main initiatives: Ibrahim Index of African Governance (IIAG); Ibrahim Forum; Ibrahim Prize for Achievement in African Leadership and Ibrahim Leadership Fellowships.

ANTONY JENKINS
("Financially Late", p. 70)

Current Role: Founder of fintech firm 10x Future Technologies and shadow chair of Institute for Apprenticeships, (UK).

Education: BA in Philosophy, Politics and Economics at Oxford University and MBA from Cranfield School of Management.

Career Snapshot: A graduate trainee at Barclays in 1983, he spent six years there before joining Citigroup, later returning to Barclays to fill a series of senior management roles in retail and corporate banking. He was the bank's chief executive from 2012 to 2015.

CRAIG KIELBURGER
("Young At Heart", p. 110)

Current Role: Humanitarian, activist, and social entrepreneur.

Education: Studied Peace and Conflict Studies at the University of Toronto before completing an Executive MBA at Schulich School of Business at York University and Kellogg School of Management at Northwestern University, (CAN).

Career Snapshot: Co-Founder of the WE Movement (WE Charity, WE Day and ME to WE social enterprises), which brings people together and gives them the tools to change the world. Craig is also a New York Times bestselling author, who has received 15 honorary degrees, the Order of Canada, the Nelson Mandela Freedom Medal and the World Children's Prize.

FRÉDÉRIC LE MANACH
("Troubled Waters", p. 42)

Current Role: Scientific director of the non profit conservation organisation, BLOOM.

Education: University of Paris (B.S), University of Plymouth (MSc), University of British Columbia, (PhD).

Career Snapshot: Alongside his work at BLOOM, Frédéric is also a member of the Marine Stewardship Council's Stakeholder Council.

DR. THOMAS LOVEJOY
("The Bite", p. 30)

Current Role: Science Envoy for the US State Department and senior fellow at the United Nations Foundation. Professor at George Mason University. Past chair of the Scientific Technical Advisory Panel for the Global Environment Facility.

Education: Millbrook School, B.S and Ph.D. in Biology from Yale University.

Career Snapshot: Worked as a tropical biologist and conservation biologist in the Amazon before directing the conservation program at World Wildlife Fund-U.S and becoming Assistant Secretary for Environmental and External Affairs for the Smithsonian Institution in Washington, D.C. He served as chief biodiversity adviser to the President of the World Bank and was the first Biodiversity Chair of the H. John Heinz III Center for Science, Economics and the Environment. He is past president of the American Institute of Biological Sciences. Awarded the Blue Planet Prize.

WILLIAM MCDONOUGH
("The Pollution Century", p. 36)

Current Role: Architect, advisor, designer, author and globally recognized leader in sustainable development. Currently serves on the World Economic Forum's Global Future Council on the Future of Environment and Natural Resource Security and advises companies and leaders worldwide through McDonough Innovation; William McDonough + Partners, architects; and MBDC, a Cradle to Cradle® consulting firm.

Education: Dartmouth College and Yale University, (USA).

Career Snapshot: Co-author of Cradle to Cradle: Remaking the Way We Make Things & The Upcycle: Beyond Sustainability – Designing for Abundance; co-founder of the Cradle to Cradle Products Innovation Institute & Make It Right; architect of many recognized flagships of sustainable design including the Ford Rouge revitalization project in Michigan and NASA's Sustainability Base in California. Served as Dean of Architecture at the University of Virginia (1994-1999); currently a consulting professor at Stanford University. Awards include the Presidential Award for Sustainable Development, the Presidential Green Chemistry Challenge Award, & the National Design Award. Time magazine has recognized him as a "Hero for the Planet".

LORD MARK MALLOCH-BROWN
("Divided Nations", p. 94)

Current Role: Chair of the Business and Sustainable Development Commission. Chairman of SGO and its elections division Smartmatic, a leading elections technology company. Sits in the House of Lords. Board member for a number of UK listed companies and chairs or is on the Board of a number of non-profit boards including the International Crisis Group and the Open Society Foundation, and a Distinguished Practitioner of the Blavatnik School of Government at Oxford University.

Education: Marlborough College. First class honours degree in history from Magdalene College, Cambridge, (UK). Masters degree in Political Science from Michigan University, (USA).

Career Snapshot: Founder of the Economist Development Report, Vice-President for External Affairs at the World Bank, Administrator UNDP, UN Deputy Secretary General, Minister of State at Foreign and Commonwealth Office. Appointed a Knight Commander of the Order of St Michael and St George.

("Troubled Waters", p. 42)

Current Role: Founder and Chair of the non profit conservation organisation, BLOOM based in Paris and Hong Kong.

Education: B.A in History, University of Paris IV Sorbonne, (FRA).

Career Snapshot: Before founding BLOOM, Claire was a journalist and produced/directed several awarded documentaries (ARTE). In 2006, she published The Deep and created the eponymous exhibition. She is a Pew Fellow in Marine Conservation since 2012, and an Ashoka Fellow since 2014 and was awarded Environmental Woman of the Year" in the 2012 "Femmes en Or" awards.

JOHN PERKINS

("Touch the Jaguar", p. 126)

Current Role: Bestselling author, board member of non profits Dream Change and The Pachamama Alliance.

Education: Graduated from the Tilton School in New Hampshire before attending Middlebury College, Vermont and later gaining a BSc in Business Administration from Boston University, (USA).

Career Snapshot: After volunteering in the Peace Corps, John became Chief Economist at Boston consulting firm, Chas T Main, advising the World Bank, the UN and the IMF. He subsequently wrote the New York Times bestseller, Confessions of an Economic Hit Man, which has been translated in to 37 languages. The book explained his part in a system that induced countries to take large loans for questionable infrastructure projects. His latest work, New Confessions of an Economic Hit Man, is out now. He has also written works on shamanism and indigenous cultures.

PAUL POLMAN

("If We Want To Go Far", p. 100)

Current Role: CEO, Unilever. Chairman, World Business Council for Sustainable Development

Education: University of Groningen (NED), University of Cincinnati, (USA).

Career Snapshot: Former executive at Procter and Gamble and Nestlé, and CEO of Unilever since January 2009. Board member, UN Global Compact and Global Consumer Goods Forum. He was a member of the High Level Panel on the creation of the UN Sustainable Development Goals (SDGs) and serves as SDG Advocate at the invitation of the UN Secretary General. Among many recognitions, he received the UN Champion of the Earth Award in 2015, the UN's highest environmental accolade. Founder and President of the Kilimanjaro Blind Trust, a foundation that benefits blind children in Africa.

JONATHON PORRITT

("Breaking Bad", p. 16)

Current Role: Environmentalist, writer and Founder Director of Forum for the Future. A non-executive director of Willmott Dixon Holdings, trustee of the Ashden Awards for Sustainable Development, he also advises a number of companies, including Marks & Spencer, and many NGOs and charities on sustainable development. He is Chancellor of Keele University, (UK).

Education: Eton College, with a First in Modern Languages from Magdalen College, University of Oxford.

Career Snapshot: Initially a teacher in West London, Jonathon became chair of the UK's Ecology Party and director of Friends of the Earth, before founding Forum for the Future and becoming inaugural chair of the UK Sustainable Development Commission. Jonathon received a CBE in January 2000 for services to environmental protection.

PROF. JOHAN ROCKSTRÖM
("Ground Control", p. 132; "The Nine Planetary Boundaries", p. 142)

Current role: Internationally recognised scientist working on global sustainability issues. Professor in Environmental Science at Stockholm University and the Director of the Stockholm Resilience Centre.

Education: PhD at Stockholm University's Systems Ecology Department, (SWE).

Career Snapshot: Expert on water resources in tropical regions. Led a team of scientists who presented the planetary boundaries framework used to help guide governments, international organisations, NGOs, and companies considering sustainable development. Author of research into agriculture systems, land use and ecosystem services. Advisor on sustainable development issues at United Nations General Assemblies, World Economic Forums, and the United Nations Framework Convention on Climate Change Conferences and chair of the advisory board for the EAT Foundation.

DAVID MAYER DE ROTHSCHILD
("The Wood For The Trees", p. 48)

Current Role: Chief Curiosity Officer of Lost Explorer and Founder of Sculpt the Future foundation.

Education: Oxford Brooks University (BSC Hon), Collage of Naturopathic Medicine, (ND).

Career Snapshot: An environmentalist and explorer, and one of the leaders of a new generation of change-makers focussed on re-igniting collective hope in the future of the planet.
Recognised as by UNEP, National Geographic, Clean up the World, the World Economic Forum and the Clinton Global Initiative as a Climate Hero, an Emerging Explorer, a Global Clean Up Ambassador, a Young Global Leader and a member of the Clinton Global Initiative Lead.

DOV SEIDMAN
("A Human Touch", p. 64)

Current Role: Founder and Chief Executive Officer of LRN, Author of New York Times best-selling book, "HOW: Why HOW We Do Anything Means Everything". Board member, 92nd Street Y.

Education: Advanced degrees in philosophy from UCLA and Oxford University and graduate of Harvard Law School.

Career Snapshot: Twenty years ago, Dov founded LRN with a powerful vision that the world would be a better place if more people did the right thing. From that basic notion, he has grown a successful business that has helped to shape the governance, culture and leadership of organizations and the way millions of employees, managers and leaders behave and interact all over the globe. Since 2007, his award-winning book HOW has been published around the world. Led by a lifelong pursuit and passion for ethical leadership, he and his company LRN became the exclusive corporate sponsors of the Elie Wiesel Foundation for Humanity Prize in Ethics.

BISHOP MARCELO SÁNCHEZ SORONDO
("Amazing Grace", p. 148)

Current Role: Argentine born Catholic bishop and Chancellor of the Pontifical Academy of Sciences and the Pontifical Academy of Social Sciences at the Vatican.

Education: Graduating summa cum laude for a Ph.D in sacred theology from the Pontifical University of St. Thomas Aquinas Rome and in Philosophy at Perugia University.

Career Snapshot: Professor in the history of philosophy at the Lateran University in Rome and Libera Università Maria SS. Assunta. Consecrated as Titular Bishop of Forum Novum (Vescovio) and a member of the Pontifical Commission for Latin America. Awarded the Légion d'Honneur of France, Cavaliere di Gran Croce of the Italian Republic, Grão Mestre da Ordem de Rio Branco of Brazil, Chaplain Grand Cross of Merit of the Sacred Military Constantinian Order of Saint George.

TOM SZAKY
("The Refuse Refusal", p. 58)

Current Role: CEO and Founder TerraCycle.

Education: Princeton University.

Career Snapshot: Hungarian born, but Canadian raised, Tom founded recycling firm Terracycle in 2001 growing it to operate across 20 countries. He was named No 1 CEO in American under 30 in 2006. He is the author of three books, including 'Revolution In A Bottle' and 'Outsmart Waste'.

PAULINE TANGIORA
("A Cultured Approach", p. 120)

Current Role: A Maori elder from the Rongomaiwahine tribe involved in supporting of Maori initiatives. Founding and current member of the World Future Council and founding member of the One Earth Institute and member Rising Women Rising World. She presents submissions on the preservation of the environment and conservation from a Maori perspective at conferences across Aotearoa and overseas, (NZ).

Education: Attended Napier Girls High School, past extra mural student Massey University, also a trained family counsellor.

Career Snapshot: A Justice of the Peace, former President and Vice President of WILPF Aotearoa, the former Regional Women's Representative for the World Council for Indigenous Peoples, Earth Charter Commissioner and a member of the Earth Council. Tangiora is a life member of the Maori Women's Welfare League and a Patron of the Peace Foundation. She has represented Aotearoa at many international fora and was a Consultant to the International Steering Committee of the World Court Project.

MPHO TUTU VAN FURTH
("A Balancing Act", p. 154)

Current Role: Human rights activist working in South Africa and the USA, where she works with vulnerable children, rape victims and refugees. Director of the Tutu Institute for Prayer and Pilgrimage, (SA).

Education: Educated at the Waterford Kamhlaba school in Swaziland.

Career Snapshot: Ordained a priest of the Episcopal Church by her father after training in the US, she was forced to resign from her post with the South African Anglican Church after marrying long-time partner Marceline van Furth.

DESMOND TUTU
("A Balancing Act", p. 154)

Current Role: Global activist for peace, democracy and human rights.

Education: Studied at the Pretoria Bantu Normal College before teaching at Johannesburg Bantu High School before studying theology at St Peter's Theological College in Rosettenville, Johannesburg, and King's College London where he received his Bachelor's and Master's degrees in theology.

Career Snapshot: The first black Archbishop of Cape Town, he became Secretary General of the South African Council of Churches, rising to international fame for leading opposition to apartheid. He received the Nobel Peace Prize in 1984; the Albert Schweitzer Prize for Humanitarianism in 1986; the Pacem in Terris Award in 1987; the Sydney Peace Prize in 1999; the Gandhi Peace Prize in 2007; and the Presidential Medal of Freedom in 2009. After the fall of apartheid he headed the Truth and Reconciliation Commission, retiring as Archbishop of Cape Town in 1996 and being made emeritus Archbishop of Cape Town, an honorary title that is unusual in the Anglican church. He is credited with coining the term 'Rainbow Nation' as a metaphor for post-apartheid South Africa after 1994 under African National Congress rule. The expression entered mainstream consciousness to describe South Africa's ethnic diversity. He announced his retirement from public life when he turned 79 in October 2010, saying: "Instead of growing old gracefully, at home with my family – reading and writing and praying and thinking – too much of my time has been spent at airports and in hotels".

STEVE WAYGOOD
("Fair Trading", p. 76)

Current Role: Chief Responsible Investment Officer, Aviva Investors.

Education: BSc (Hons) Economics, a PhD in Sustainable Finance and the CFA Society of the UK's Investment Management Certificate.

Career Snapshot: Founded the Sustainable Stock Exchange Initiative. A faculty member at the International Corporate Governance Network as well as the University of Cambridge Institute for Sustainability Leadership. He received a Leadership in Sustainability award from the Corporation of London in 2013 and the Yale Rising Star in Corporate Governance Award in 2011.

STELLA WHEILDON
("In the Beginning", p. 124)

Current Role: Stella works to empower the ancient traditions of the Ngarakbal and their connection to all tribal nations of the earth.

Education: From a very young age, she listened and learned the Aboriginal stories from her Komilaroi grandmother. Instilling a strong and vital connection to Nature and interest in the historical, mystical and physical lore's of the ancient oral indigenous wisdom traditions.

Career Snapshot: In 1998 Stella commenced an environmental campaign to defend the sacred mountain Wollumbin from industrial mining and deforestation and has worked closely with the Ngarakbal and its marriage clan the Githabal peoples, she is the author of numerous books.

PROF. MUHAMMAD YUNUS
("We've Jobs", p. 106)

Current Role: Former Nobel Peace Prize Winner. Bangladeshi social entrepreneur, banker, economist, and civil society leader. Co-founder of Yunus Social Business – Global Initiatives empowering social businesses to address and solve social problems around the world.

Education: Matriculated from Chittagong Collegiate School ranking 16th of 39,000 students in East Pakistan. BA and MA in Economics at Dhaka University. Received Fulbright scholarship to study in the United States. Ph.D in economics from the Vanderbilt University Graduate Program in Economic Development.

Career Snapshot: Professor and head of economics at Chittagong University, publisher of Bangladesh Newspaper, introduced village government programme, before founding the Grameen Bank and pioneering the concepts of microcredit and microfinance. Awarded the Nobel Prize, the United States Presidential Medal of Freedom and the Congressional Gold Medal.

PUBLISHERS

KIM POLMAN
("A New Golden Era", p. 8)

Current Role: Founder and Chair of the Board of Trustees, Reboot the Future.

Education: MA in Arts Administration from the University of Cincinnati, Conservatory of Music.

Career Snapshot: Started her professional life in Arts Management, before moving around Europe raising three sons with her husband. She oversees a charity dedicated to literacy for the blind and visually impaired in Africa.

STEPHEN VASCONCELLOS-SHARPE
("A New Golden Era", p. 8)

Current Role: Founder and CEO of Reboot the Future. Publisher of Salt magazine, a platform for change agents and transformational leadership.

Education: LLB Hons in Law from University of Edinburgh.

Career Snapshot: Serial entrepreneur and committed change agent. Formerly CEO of Country Strategic, a company specialised in nation-branding, with a record of working at the highest level in over 60 countries worldwide.

BIBLIOGRAPHY

A Long Way Gone, Ishmael Beah, Sarah Crichton Books, (2008).

C.G Jung, Collected Works, Volume 7, Routledge, (1953).

Cradle to Cradle: Remaking the Way We Make Things, Michael Braungart and William McDonough, Farrar, Straus and Giroux. (2002).

Eternal Treblinka by Charles Patterson, Lantern Books, (2002).

Free The Children, Craig Kielburger, Kevin Major, Harper Perennial, (1999).

Half Earth, Edward O. Wilson, Liveright, (2016).

How: Why HOW We Do Anything Means Everything, Dov Seidman, John Wiley & Sons, (2007).

Love Letter To The Earth, Thich Nhat Hanh, Parallax Press, (2013).

New Confessions of an Economic Hitman, John Perkins, Berrett-Koehler, (2016).

The Autobiography of Upton Sinclair, Harcourt, Brace & World, (1962).

The Book of Kells, (c.800).

The Dream of Earth, Thomas Berry, Sierra Club Books, (1988).

The Empathic Civilization: The Race to Global Consciousness in a World in Crisis By Jeremy Rifkin, Jeremy Tarcher, (2010).

The Jungle, Upton Sinclair, Doubleday, (1906).

The Tales of Sendebar, (c 1200).

The Universe is a Green Dragon, Brian Swimme, Bear and Company, (1984).

The Wealth of Nations by Adam Smith, William Strahan and Thomas Cadell, (1776).

The World We Made, Jonathon Porritt, Phaidon, (2013).

ORGANISATIONS CITED BY AUTHORS

Aviva – *aviva.com*

Bloom – *bloomassociation.org*

Business and Sustainable Development Commission – *business commission.org*

Carbon Pricing Leadership Coalition to the Taskforce for Climate related Financial Disclosures – *carbonpricingleadership.org*

Center for Compassion and Altruism Research and Education – *ccare.stanford.edu*

Children's Birthday Miracles – *childrensbirthdaymiracles.com*

Desmond and Leah Tutu Legacy Foundation – *tutu.org.za*

Dream Change – *dreamchange.org*

Ellen MacArthur Foundation – *ellenmacarthurfoundation.org*

Fairtrade Foundation – *fairtrade.org.uk*

Findhorn Foundation – *findhorn.org*

Forum for the Future – *forumforthefuture.org*

Global Consumer Good Forum – *theconsumergoodsforum.com*

Global Financial Integrity – *gfintegrity.org*

Grameen – *grameenfoundation.org*

I Love Me Club – *ilovemeclub.org*

Ibrahim Index of African Governance – *mo.ibrahimfoundation*

Integrated Reporting Framework – *integratedreporting.org*

LRN – *lrn.com*

Mission Measurement – *missionmeasurement.com*

Natural Capital Protocol – *naturalcapitalcoalition.org*

Pachamama Alliance – *pachamama.org*

Paris Climate Agreement – *unfccc.int/paris_agreement*

Salum Shamte – *actanzania.or.tz*

South Asian Coalition on Child Servitude – *bba.org*

Stella Wheildon – *stellawheildon.com*

Stockholm Resilience Centre – *stockholmresilience.org*

Sustainable Accounting Standards – *sasb.org*

Terracycle – *terracycle.com*

The Chinese Association of the Circular Economy – *chinacace.org*

The Global Reporting Initiative – *globalreporting.org*

The HeartMath Institute – *heartmath.org*

The International Organisation for Standardisation – *iso.org*

The International Slavery Museum, Liverpool – *liverpoolmuseums.org*

The Lost Explorer – *lostexplorer.com*

The Woods Hole Research Centre, Falmouth, Massachusetts – *whrc.org*

Tropical Forest Alliance – *tfa2020.org*

UN Foundation – *unfoundation.org*

Unilever Sustainable Living Plan – *unilever.com*

United Nations Sustainable Development Goals – *undp.org*

WE – *we.org*

William McDonough + Partners – *mcdonoughpartners.com*

World Business Council for Sustainable Development – *wbcsd.com*

World Economic Forum – *weforum.org*

Yunus Social Business – *yunussb.com*

JOURNALS, SCIENTIFIC PAPERS AND OTHER REFERENCES CITED BY AUTHORS

Cashion et al. 2016 (in review) *Global fishmeal production over the last 60 years: why are we grinding up food-grade fish?*

FAO (2016) *The state of world fisheries and aquaculture* - Contributing to food security and nutrition for all. Food and Agriculture Organization of the United Nations (FAO), Rome (Italy). x + 190 p FAO (2008) FAOSTAT. Food and Agriculture Organization of the United Nations, FAO), Rome (Italy). Available at: http://faostat.fao.org/.

Grow Africa: Partnering to Achieve African Agriculture Transformation. World Economic Form in collaboration with A.T. Kearney, January 2016

Golden Rule Chronology, http://www.harryhiker.com/chronology.htm

Hodal et al. (2014) *Revealed: Asian slave labour producing prawns for supermarkets in US, UK.* The Guardian, edition of June 10 2014.

Huxley (1885) *Inaugural address.* pp. 80-90 In. Fisheries Exhibition Literature Scientific Memoirs 5

McCraty, R., Atkinson, M., Tomasino, D., & Bradley, R. T (2009). *"The coherent heart: Heart-brain interactions, psychophysiological coherence, and the emergence of system-wide order."* Integral Review 5(2): 10-115.

McCraty, R., et al. (2012). *"The global coherence initiative: creating a coherent planetary standing wave."* Glob Adv Health Med 1(1): 64-77

McCraty, R. and M. Zayas (2014). *"Intuitive Intelligence, Self-regulation, and Lifting Consciousness."* Glob Adv Health Med 3(2): 56-65.

McCraty, R. (2015). *The Energetic Heart: Biomagnetic Communication Within and Between People.* Bioelectromagnetic and Subtle Energy Medicine, Second Edition. P. J. Rosch.

McCraty, R. and A. Deyhle (2015). *The Global Coherence Initiative: Investigating the Dynamic Relationship* between *People and Earth's Energetic Systems Bioelectromagnetic and Subtle Energy Medicine,* Second Edition. P. J. Rosch.

McCraty, R. (2016). *Science of The Heart* Vol.2. Boulder Creek, Ca, HeartMath Institute

Morris, S. M. (2010). *"Facilitating collective coherence: Group Effects on Heart Rate Variability Coherence and Heart Rhythm Synchronization."* Alternative Therapies in Health and Medicine 16(4): 62-72.

Pauly (2013) *Does catch reflect abundance? Yes, it is a crucial signal.* Nature 494(7437): 303-306.

Roadmap for Sustainable Capital Markets - available on line at www.aviva.com/roadmap

Scharmer, O. and K. Kaufer (2013) *"Leading from the Emerging Future: From Ego-System to Eco-System Economies: Applying Theory U to Transforming Business, Society and Self"* Berrett-Koehler Publishers, San Francisco: USA

Rockström et al. 2009 *A Safe Operating Space For Humanity.* Nature 471. 472-475

Steffen et al. 2015. *Planetary Boundaries: Guiding human development on a changing planet.* Science Vol. 347 no. 6223.

'U.Lab: Leading from the Emerging Future' MOOC see https://www.edx.org

Wickens (2016) *How vital fish stocks in Africa are being stolen from human mouths to feed pigs and chickens on Western factory farms.* The Independent, edition of September 19, 2016